MARESFIELD LIBRARY

IMAGINATION AND REALITY

Psycho-Analytical Essays
1951–1961

CHARLES RYCROFT

INTRODUCTION BY
M. MASUD R. KHAN
AND
JOHN D. SUTHERLAND

MARESFIELD LIBRARY
LONDON

Reprinted 1987 with permission of
Hogarth Press Ltd by
H. Karnac (Books) Ltd,
58 Gloucester Road,
London SW7
England

ISBN 0 946439 35 4

Printed and bound in Great Britain by
A. Wheaton & Co. Ltd, Exeter

Contents

v

Introduction

Having discovered the pervasive effects of the unconscious and of infantile sexuality, Freud founded the psycho-analytical movement which would, he hoped, provide an organization of individuals supra-personal and supra-national in their dedication to the new science of psycho-analysis. However even at the outset, as his difficulties with Jung and the Swiss school of analysts showed, it became apparent that psycho-analysis would be influenced by the languages and national climates of its new adherents, and it was indeed only natural that new inflections of emphasis and different biases of interest would manifest themselves in other countries in which psycho-analysis took root.

In the spread of the psycho-analytic movement, perhaps in no other country has psycho-analysis found more solid adherents than in Great Britain, and yet perhaps nowhere else has the native genius and style of a people so influenced the character of psycho-analytic theory and practice as in the work and researches of the members of the British Psycho-Analytical Society. One has to mention only a few names to establish the verity of this statement, for example those of Ernest Jones, Sylvia Payne, Edward Glover, John Rickman, James Strachey, J. C. Flugel, and Ella Sharpe before the war and those of Fairbairn, Winnicott, W. C. M. Scott, Marjorie Brierley, John Bowlby, and Marion Milner after it. A unique feature of the development of the British Society has been its capacity to include such outstanding personages as Melanie Klein and Anna Freud and assimilate their creative thought without losing the character of its own empirical and catholic tradition.

It is in this characteristic British tradition that Dr Charles Rycroft was nurtured and found his own definitive style of thought and clinical work. One can single out some features from this very complex structure of clinical sensibility and theoretical thinking. Perhaps its most striking characteristic is an empiricism that addresses itself to the study of the total

person in the clinical setting. Reading Dr Rycroft's papers on
technique one is immediately struck by the patient as a person
on the one hand and the extreme sensitivity to the imaginative
and psychic processes of which language is *par excellence* the
vehicle on the other. He conceives of language not merely as a
technical idiom for transcribing instinctual derivatives, but
rather as the vehicle of imaginative processes which articulate
the whole being, and shares with Ella Sharpe, Winnicott, and
Marion Milner an acute awareness of the rôle played by the
imagination at every level of mental functioning. One consequence of this emphasis on imagination is a shift from considering inner life as a self-sealed unit to that of evaluating the total
experience of the patient as a person and his affectivity in terms
of his cultural reality and its tradition.

From the very beginning of psycho-analytic researches the
tendency has been towards a split between those who empha-
sized the sovereignty of the internal process and those that
rather over-simplified and exaggerated the rôle of current social
factors, the latter being exemplified by the work of Karen
Horney and Eric Fromm, etc. In the researches of the group of
analysts who have been working in the climate of the British
Society, one sees an attempt to find the bridge between these
two extreme simplifications of the human situation. If the
human individual on the one hand is instinct-ridden and his
whole character is formed by this exigency, he is on the other
hand object-anchored. Thus his inner world draws directly
upon the cultural climate with all the richness and prejudices
that his adult environment brings to his nurture through their
care of him as a child. The human faculty which enables this
dialogic process to take place between the inner and the outer,
the instinctive and the social, the private and the public Self,
is the imaginative faculty. Dr Rycroft's papers address themselves primarily to an examination, definition and clarification
of the rôle of imagination and reality, both in the clinical process and in the total developmental life-space of the individual
and his maturation into a person.

Dr Rycroft took a degree in history at Cambridge. Then his
intellectual curiosity and interest bought him to psycho-analysis
and medicine. In the two decades following the war Dr Rycroft
has played a significant and important rôle both in the institu-
tional affairs of the British Society as well as in its scientific and
academic pursuits. This collection of his papers testifies not only

INTRODUCTION

to his singular sensitivity and talent as an analyst but it also reflects the climate of intellectual thought and clinical research typical of the British school of psycho-analysis during these decades.

M. MASUD R. KHAN AND J. D. SUTHERLAND

May 1967

IMAGINATION AND REALITY

A Contribution to the Study of the Dream Screen[1]

INTRODUCTION

In this paper I wish to report an example of a dream without visual content of the type described by Lewin in his paper, 'Sleep, the Mouth and the Dream Screen' (1946), and to make some suggestions as to the clinical and theoretical significance of such dreams.

In his second paper on the dream screen Lewin (1948) writes:

> The dream screen is defined as the blank background upon which the dream picture appears to be projected. The term was suggested by the motion picture, because, like its analogue in the cinema, the dream screen is either not noted by the dreaming spectator, or it is ignored due to the interest in the pictures and action that appear on it. However in certain circumstances the screen plays a rôle of its own and becomes perceptible. . . .

Like other formal elements in dreams the screen has a meaning in itself. It

> represents the idea of 'sleep'; it is the element of the dream that betokens the fulfilment of the cardinal wish to sleep, which Freud considered responsible for all dreaming. Also it represents the maternal breast, usually flattened out, as the infant might perceive it while falling asleep. It appears to be the equivalent or the continuation in sleep, of the breast hallucinated in certain predormescent states, occasionally observed in adults (Isakower, 1938).

Dreams occur which have as their visual element the dream screen alone, without any superimposed dream picture. Such

[1] First published in the *Int. J. Psycho-Anal.* (1951), **32.**

dreams represent 'complete fulfilments of the wish to sleep at the maternal breast after nursing'.

Lewin's papers are primarily concerned with demonstrating the existence of the dream screen, and with discussing its theoretical significance in relation to the general theory of dreams and the psychology of sleep. I intend in this paper to approach the subject from a rather different angle, by giving a fuller analysis of an individual dream of this kind than has been attempted by Lewin. I intend, also, to suggest possible answers to two closely connected clinical questions which arise from the recognition of such dreams. First, at what stage in an analysis are dreams in which the dream screen is visible likely to occur? Secondly, what dynamic process in the patient does their occurrence represent? The answer to the more general question as to the type of patient in which these dreams are likely to be observed is explicit in Lewin's formulation. It is in those with deep oral fixations, whose paramount wish is for union with the breast.

CLINICAL MATERIAL

My patient's dream was as follows: 'It felt as though you [the analyst] had taken me under your wing. There was nothing to see in the dream at all. It was like a white sheet.' After telling me the dream he pointed out explicitly that the feeling he had had that I was taking him under my wing was a metaphorical description of the affect colouring the dream and not part of its visual content. He also remarked that he was not happy in describing the dream as a white sheet, but that it was the best he could do to convey the peculiar impression that the dream had made. He gave three immediate associations. First, he had had the same experience, including the awareness of a white sheet of light, during the previous analytical session, but had thought it too silly to mention. Secondly, the night of the dream had been the best night's sleep he could ever remember having had. Thirdly, the dream had recurred three or four times during the night.

In order to understand this dream it is necessary to know something of, first, the patient's history and symptoms, and, secondly, the analytical work preceding and following the dream.

The patient was a married man of 45. He was several years younger than any of his brothers and sisters, two of whom committed suicide following depressive illnesses. His mother was a

2

dominating character, whom he alternately feared and idealized. I have the impression that she was a woman who resented her children growing up and who could love them only so long as they were totally dependent on her. There is no direct evidence about breast-feeding and weaning, though I am inclined to believe that my patient was correct in his belief that he was weaned ràther late. His father was a kindly, meek, unassuming man, who was often away from home.

He had, when he came to analysis, next to no belief in his own masculinity. He was virtually impotent, had a deep sense of guilt about masturbation, suffered from headaches, attacks of giddiness with vomiting closely resembling Ménière's Disease, psychogenic deafness and short sight, and complained of feelings of unreality in his arms and legs, which on occasion felt as though they had swollen to two or three times their real size. From early on in the analysis it was clear that his sense of guilt centred on his unconscious hostility to his mother. His masturbation, which was without conscious fantasy, represented an attack on her, both in terms of defiance of her prohibitions and of urinary attack. (As a child he had been enuretic.) It also represented a rejection of her and of women in general. His visual and auditory symptoms constituted defences against scopophilic and listening interests, which had the unconscious significance of oral-sadistic incorporation. The feelings of unreality in his limbs represented defences against wishes to hit and kick.

His giddiness differed from his other symptoms in the fact that the sadism was uppermost, whereas in his other symptoms the defence against sadism was most apparent. Fundamentally it represented the wish that his internalized mother should disintegrate. He once said jokingly: 'Everything was going round so fast that I wonder the house didn't fall down.' The previous night he had dreamt that an engineer had told him that almost the whole house would have to be pulled down before electricity could be installed. Here the house clearly symbolized not only his ego, which he felt to be in need of almost complete reconstruction before he could achieve potency, but also, or, rather, more specifically, that part of his ego which had been formed by introjection of his mother (Schilder, 1930).

In addition to their oral-sadistic significance these symptoms had also a genital, sexual meaning. For instance, the swelling of his limbs symbolized erection and was related to a feeling that his penis was abnormally small. The giddiness represented

3

orgasm as well as a wish to destroy his introjected mother. The worst attack he ever had, with frequent vomiting during the analytical hour, was precipitated by the expectation of an outstanding professional success. The symptom began after he had achieved promotion out of an occupation which his father had practised for many years without any advancement. However, during the part of the analysis with which we are concerned here, the important, dynamic interpretations were undoubtedly those given at the oral level.

His relation to his wife was profoundly disturbed by projection of the maternal imago on to her. Consciously he idealized her and thought her perfect, but he suffered from compulsive wishes to be catty and sarcastic to her, while his symptoms served the purpose of preventing her enjoying herself and compelling her to look after him. Attempts at sexual intercourse were disturbed by visual images of his mother intruding themselves on his image of his wife.

In general, the analysis of his symptoms led to three conclusions. First, the symptoms were a defence against guilt and depression about his hostility to his mother. Secondly, he was orally dependent on her. In this connexion it is significant that he had sucked his thumb all his life. This dependence expressed itself during the analysis as a dependence on his wife and on me. Thirdly, he had attempted to resolve his difficulties with his mother by identification with her. His relationships both with his wife and with me were based on a narcissistic identification. His attitude to me was that he defended himself against having any feelings about me. He took my interpretations and worked on them himself, without allowing them to become part of an object-relationship existing between us. In other words, he tried to be his own analyst.

As regards the relation of his symptoms to depression, it was very striking how circumstances, which prior to the analysis would have made him deaf or giddy, came later to make him depressed. He once made the interesting comment that depression with insight into its causes is more tolerable than symptoms. The operative phrase there was, I think, 'with insight'.

As a result of the identification with his mother passive homosexual feelings were important. Yearnings for the breast and mother were displaced on to the penis and father-figures. Wishes to look at the male genital were particularly strong, and he could remember thinking as a child that his father's penis

4

was a sort of breast. His dominant infantile theory of sexual intercourse was undoubtedly fellatio. This displacement from breast to penis is important in the material leading up to the dream screen dream.

By a fortnight before the dream, which occurred in the tenth month of analysis, he had acquired a large measure of genuine insight into his problems and was clearly conscious of the mixture of hostility, dependence and identification that characterized his relationship with his wife. In relation to me, however, he had no conscious feelings and was clearly defending himself against the possibility of feeling dependent on me. The relatively superficial reasons for this were, first, that he feared my impending holidays, and, secondly, the homosexual implications of being dependent on a male analyst. From a deeper point of view it was due to a fear of hostility, both his own and mine. It so happened that at this time he had to go out of London for two days in the middle of the week, and, for the first time since the beginning of the analysis, he was separated from both his wife and me at the same time. His giddiness and deafness returned while he was away, and on his first night back in London he had the following dream: 'You gave me a bottle of Schnapps. The bottle was of a curious shape and had two different fluids in it. One of them was milk. I was too embarrassed by the gift to thank you.' I interpreted this dream as showing his unconscious oral dependence on me, a dependence he had been denying while he was away. This interpretation was accepted only intellectually, and the analysis turned to the question of why he had been too embarrassed to thank me.

He told me his behaviour in the dream was characteristic of him. He found it difficult to accept gifts, or, indeed, offered pleasures of any kind. This was due not so much to a sense of guilt as to a feeling that acceptance put him in the power of the donor. He was particularly frightened of being tantalized. He had the feeling that if he admitted to wanting anything it would immediately be taken away from him. In other words, he was unable to accept a 'good' external object for fear that it would turn out to be 'bad' and hostile. Experiences of being teased contributed to this fear, but fundamentally it was related to a projection of his own wishes to frustrate, as was shown by the habit, which he had at this time, of tantalizing me by telling me at the beginning of each hour that he had dreamt the previous night but could not remember the dream. In doing this he was using dreams as such to represent breasts and frustrating me in the same way as he felt his mother had frustrated him.

The unconscious oral longings for the analyst as a 'good' external object were also shown by an hallucination which he had at this time. He was in church, and while listening to the lesson he distinctly saw the reader's penis with urine flowing from it. The connexion here between urinary flow and speech — means by which the analyst gives himself to the patient — left no doubt that this experience represented an attempt at hallucinatory fulfilment of oral longings for the analyst. This interpretation was confirmed by the facility he displayed at this time in seeing resemblances to the penis in various cracks and shadows on the consulting-room wall. This hallucination, as well as others which occurred during the early part of the analysis, should really be described as a pseudo-hallucination, since it was immediately dismissed as absurd, even though it had all the vividness of a true perception.

The dream screen dream occurred at this juncture. In the light of the preceding material its meaning was fairly clear. It represented the successful fulfilment in sleep of the wish for oral union with the analyst, who was taking the rôle of the mother's breast (and the father's penis conceived of as a breast). This oral union was an external object-relationship, and the real importance of the dream was that it marked the shift from a narcissistic attitude of identification with an internal object to one of turning towards an external object, even though the external object still bore the projected imago of the fantasied breast. The analyst was accepted as a helping, protecting figure — 'it felt as though you had taken me under your wing' — instead of his being someone who had to be kept at a distance for fear of his turning out to be threatening and dangerous.

Although from this dream we may assume an advance, the underlying fantasy of union with the mother had also an important defensive function. As described later, the establishment of an object-relationship with the analyst necessitated his using various manic mechanisms, which enabled him to deny the existence of guilt about hostility to his mother. The dream was not simply a wish-fulfilment of his oral longings; it represented in addition a defensive merging of the ego and super-ego, a process which, according to Rado (1928), 'is the faithful intrapsychic repetition of that fusing with the mother that takes place during drinking at her breast.'

6

The fact that the night of the dream was the best night's sleep he could ever remember having had was the result of the relinquishment of his narcissistic attitude. There was considerable material to show that sleep, of which he had an unusually great need, represented for him a defensive regression to a state of narcissism rather than a normal psycho-physiological satisfaction. He slept more the worse his symptoms were and could, indeed, fall asleep while feeling giddy. He always slept in the intra-uterine posture, and when upset sucked his thumb while falling asleep. One night, when he might well have been disturbed by his wife's restlessness, he dreamt that a cat was purring—a very apt symbol for a state of narcissistic withdrawal. In just the same way as sexual intercourse is more satisfying than masturbation and feeding at the breast is more nourishing than sucking a thumb, so the change from a narcissistic orientation to an object-seeking one led to a change in the quality of his sleep and an increase in the satisfaction he derived from it. (Cf. Stone's (1947) distinction between narcissistic sleep based on 'refusal or inability to nurse at the breast' and normal sleep resulting from oral gratification.)

The experience of seeing a white sheet identical with the dream screen during the previous analytical session was not especially noted at the time, except as confirmation of the view that the screen in the dream referred to the analyst. Its theoretical significance, to which I shall return later, would seem to lie in the fact that it was a 'blank' hallucination which occurred after an hallucination with visual content and before a dream without visual content.

The fact that the dream was dreamt three or four times during the night is interesting in view of Lewin's (1948) conclusion that the repetition of dreams may refer to multiple or interrupted feeds. Another determinant was, probably, that the dream occured on a Sunday night, that is, three nights after his last session with the analyst.

The interpretation of this dream as representing the abandonment of an attitude of narcissistic identification with his mother was confirmed by the further progress of the analysis. In the same hour as he told me the dream he described a change in his feeling towards me, a change which he expressed in terms of 'thinking of you as a human being for the first time'. A week later I took a fortnight's holiday, and on my return he reported that he had felt very well during my absence. This he attributed, quite correctly, to his having been able to admit missing me. He also reported two dreams which he had had during the holiday. The first was that he was his father and yet was himself too. He, or his father, had an erect penis, of which he was frightened. This clearly meant that he was sufficiently free of his maternal identification to wish to take up a masculine position, but that his fear of his mother still made such a position untenable.

In the second dream the dream screen was again visible, though this time visual elements were superimposed upon it. It consisted of 'a canvas, or perhaps a cinema screen, which was somehow also one of the walls of the consulting-room. On it were depicted all the things that I wanted to tell you when you came back from your holidays. But the only detail I can remember clearly was a submarine in dock. The water was running out of the dock and by the end of the dream the submarine was high and dry.' There were several associations. He had in fact visited a submarine a few days before, and, although it was in harbour, had feared that it might submerge while he was in it. As a child he had lived near the sea and a recurrent anxiety of his had been that he might be drowned by a tidal wave coming in from the sea. The fear he had then as a child he recognized as similar to moments of panic he had experienced in adult life when surrounded by a surging crowd. His last and most revealing association was that while attempting sexual intercourse the previous evening he had felt his mother's power over him receding like an ebbing tide. The dream was therefore a pictorial representation of liberation from his internal mother, a liberation which was not entirely welcome, for the phrase 'high and dry' referred to a feeling which another patient of mine, rather similarly placed, called 'the limbo of being neither male nor female.'

The form of this dream supports Lewin's view that the dream screen represents the breast during sleep while 'the visual elements . . . represent the psychic elements disturbing the wish for sleep'. The things that he wanted to tell me about were the things that were disturbing him during my absence, and which, if he had had the opportunity of telling to me, would have enabled his relationship to me to be maintained without frustration.

As was to be expected, the establishment of the analyst as a 'good' external object necessitated the use of the mechanism of idealization. The threat of an impending account led him to dream of me as Sir Stafford Cripps. His associations failed to establish any connexion between the Chancellor of the Exchequer and demands for money. They were concerned entirely with his indifference to worldly things and the frugality of his personal life. The analyst had to be above worldly things, like the angel that at some periods of his childhood he had imagined in his mother. Without this idealization he would have had to contend with an analyst as avaricious and demanding as, at other periods, he had felt his mother to be.

The further progress of the analysis had no direct bearing on the problem of the dream screen, though in retrospect it was clear that the period of the screen dream had been a turning point in his development. After the dream several of his symptoms ceased entirely, e.g. his attacks of giddiness and his tendency to hallucination. He lost his capacity for defensive sleep, and there was no recurrence of narcissistic defences against the transference. As foreshadowed in his dream of being his father, the analysis became increasingly concerned with genital problems. It was found that considerable genital development had, in fact, occurred, and that the early part of the analysis had been dealing with a partial regression to the oral level following traumata at the genital.

THEORETICAL DISCUSSION

The material presented in the previous section can be summarized as follows: A visually blank dream of the kind described by Lewin occurred during the analysis of a patient with oral fixations. Its occurrence marked the renunciation of a state of narcissistic identification with his mother and cathexis of the analyst as an external object. This re-orientation involved projection of the internalized mother on to the analyst, who was idealized as a defence against fear of her hostility. The change marked an advance, since it enabled the patient to progress towards genital identification with his father, while the change in the quality of the transference made accessible anxieties associated with his infantile object-relationships. The dream represented the fulfilment in fantasy of oral longings for the analyst, and the establishment of an object-relationship with him.

Any importance these observations may have rests in the possibility that screen dreams typically have a significance of this kind. The clinical data given by Lewin do not lend them-

9

selves to any detailed comparison of his example of a pure screen dream and mine. The bare facts of his case do, however, suggest that some similar process was in operation. His patient was a schizophrenic girl. Her illness began with a stupor, and on four separate occasions she had what she called a 'no dream' accompanied by genital orgasm. Each dream followed a satisfying experience consisting of a meal and shopping expedition with a mother-substitute and heralded the onset of a hypomanic phase, during which she had erotically satisfying delusions. Lewin, following Abraham (1924), interprets both the orgasms and the delusions as primarily oral in origin, despite their expression in genital terms. Although orally fixated, my patient was certainly not schizophrenic, and, even if it were possible, any detailed comparison of the two cases would involve a discussion of the diagnostic problems raised by my patient which would go beyond the scope of this paper. Despite this, it is perhaps possible to discern an analogous process occurring in the two cases. My patient's dream marked a change from a neurotic narcissistic state to object-cathexis, while Lewin's patient's dream marked a change from a psychotic narcissistic state to a hypomanic one, in which hallucinated, projected objects were treated as real and satisfying. The difference between the two would seem to lie in the fact that my patient's capacity for discriminating between external reality and fantasy was unimpaired, as a result of which the projection of internal objects led to the development of a positive transference, which could be analysed, whereas in Lewin's case it led to delusion.

The question naturally arises as to whether my patient's condition after the dream was in any way manic. Psychiatrically speaking, this was, so far as I could observe, not the case, and there were no signs of over-activity or elation. For the next few months, however, he expressed hatred of his mother and had dreams of her dying—in reality, she had died many years previously—without any conscious guilt or remorse, and interpretations of material which suggested the presence of unconscious guilt met with no apparent response. This denial of psychical reality was made possible by the idealized nature of his positive transference, which made anger with the analyst inconceivable, and by the presence of various omnipotent fantasies, which made him feel immune from frustration and attack by his mother. These fantasies reached consciousness in terms of an unrealistically optimistic attitude to money and became accessible through the analysis of fears that a mother-substitute would make excessive financial demands upon him. The analysis of these fears led to conscious feelings of remorse and wishes to make amends for the unhappiness his neurosis had caused his family. He presented, in fact, a picture corresponding closely to that described by Melanie Klein (1935) as characteristic of the 'manic position' taken up as a defence against guilt and paranoid anxieties. The fact that his behaviour was in no way hypomanic is, like his development of a positive transference, attributable to the integrity of his capacity for reality-testing. The co-existence of omnipotent fantasies and a well-developed sense of reality seems to have been largely responsible for his success as a business man. He was able to take financial risks which most people would have considered unjustified by the circumstances, and then compensated for his rashness by a very realistic handling of the situations into which it had led him.

It is now possible to suggest an answer to the questions posed at the beginning of this paper. Dreams showing the dream screen are likely to occur when patients with narcissistic fixations are attempting to re-establish emotional contact with the external world. This attempt may be successful, as would appear to have been the case with my patient, or unsuccessful, as in Lewin's. (Lewin (1949) specifically draws attention to his patient's complete inaccessibility during her hypomanic states.) In either case the mechanism employed is projection or externalization, a mechanism which, as first described by Freud (1911), represents an attempt to re-cathect the external world. The prototype of this process is probably the moment, to which Winnicott (1945) has drawn attention, when the hungry infant projects the hallucinated breast on to the real one. There are three possible outcomes to this superimposition of hallucinated on to real object. First, the real object may be accepted as satisfying, in which case there is a shift of cathexis from the hallucinated object to the real one. In so far as this happens, the cumulative effect of repeated satisfying experiences will be to strengthen the ego's capacity to cathect the external world and lay the foundations for the development of a sense of reality. The tendency to hallucinate the object in periods of frustration will gradually be replaced by the capacity to fantasy about a memory of it. Secondly, the real object may be rejected, in which case the hallucinated object continues to be cathected. This is, one

11

surmises, what happens in the case of those anxious, over-excited infants, who, as described by Ribble (1943), for example, become stuporous when offered the breast. This is an outcome the repetition of which over any extended period of time is incompatible with life, but insofar as it occurs, it must militate against the establishment of a firm cathexis of the external world and predispose to states of withdrawal. Thirdly, the real object is partially accepted, so that both the hallucinated and the real object are cathected. In this case a split in the ego takes place, one part continuing to cathect the hallucinated object and remaining fixated on it, the other cathecting the real, external object and capable of further development. Whether or not my patient sucked his thumb while at the breast, like the babies referred to by Winnicott, his ability simultaneously to hallu-cinate objects and to dismiss them as unreal suggests the pre-sence in his ego of a split of this kind, dating from the period when the sense of reality is being established.

In this connexion the series of events—(a) hallucination of a penis, (b) hallucination of a white sheet of light during an analytical session, (c) screen dream, and (d) dream with visual elements superimposed on the screen—becomes significant. It reproduced in the analysis the series—(a) hallucination of the breast by the hungry infant, (b) superimposition of the hallu-cinated breast on to the real one, (c) cathexis of the breast, and (d) the retention in memory of a fantasy of the breast. The cathexis of the analyst as a 'good' external object made hallu-cinatory fulfilment of his oral longings unnecessary, and hence-forth hallucination was replaced by conscious feelings of depen-dence on the analyst. The second screen dream, in which 'all the things I wanted to tell you' were depicted on the screen, was related to a conscious wish for the analyst's return from holiday and represented the fulfilment in sleep of the fantasy of being reunited with him in the analytical session. Since the capacity to hallucinate was possessed by only part of his ego, the other part being capable of rejecting the hallucinations as unreal, the loss of the capacity to hallucinate marked the reuniting of a split in the ego and the achievement by the whole ego of that stage in development at which hallucination is replaced by fantasy.

My main purpose in this chapter has been to make a clinical contribution to the problem of the dream screen by reporting in some detail the psycho-analytical context in which a blank dream occured. My observations suggest that it may be possible to make two additions to Lewin's interpretation of these dreams as representing 'complete fulfilments of the wish to sleep at the maternal breast after nursing'. First, the fantasy of having fulfilled the wish to sleep at the breast represents an attempt to re-establish an object-relationship with the mother, an attempt which may, as in my patient, be successful and lead to an advance in ego-development. Secondly, this fantasy has a defensive function, since it enables anxieties associated with frustration at the breast to be denied.

Some Observations on a Case of Vertigo[1]

At the age of 45 a married man, who despite lifelong neurotic difficulties had always enjoyed excellent physical health, began to suffer from attacks of vertigo, in which the world appeared to be rotating on a vertical plane in front of him. During and intermittently between attacks he was deaf in his left ear and suffered from tinnitus. Some attacks lasted only a few minutes, others for as long as twenty-four hours. The more severe ones were accompanied by vomiting and signs of vasomotor collapse. When he was examined by an otologist the only demonstrable physical signs were slight middle-ear deafness on the left side, insufficient to account for the degree of deafness subjectively experienced, and a perforated left ear-drum, which was presumed to be the result of otitis media in childhood. The occurrence of the classical triad of symptoms, vertigo, deafness, and tinnitus in association with typical physical signs, led to a diagnosis of Ménière's Disease being made.

A year later, for reasons apparently unconnected with his attacks of vertigo, he was referred to me for analysis. Fairly soon after beginning treatment it became clear to both of us that the attacks formed an integral part of his neurosis and that the vertigo, tinnitus, and deafness all had a psychological meaning.

By this I do not mean that they were purely psychological phenomena lacking any organic basis. There were, on the contrary, several reasons for supposing that the vertigo at least was a physiological event, presumably due to central, psychic stimuli acting on a hyper-sensitive inner ear. He certainly suffered all the usual physiological concomitants and after-effects of true vertigo, such as vomiting and pallor, and although a

---

[1] This paper was read to a meeting of the British Psycho-Analytical Society on 1 October 1952 and first published in the *Int. J. Psycho-Anal.* (1953), **34.** (The clinical material is from the same patient as that in my 1951 paper, published as Chapter 1 in this volume, and there is therefore some unavoidable repetition.)

certain psychological state was a necessary pre-condition for an attack, the immediate precipitating factor was often a physical stimulus such as blowing his nose violently. His physiological threshold for vertigo was undoubtedly unusually low, but vertigo-inducing stimuli produced only momentary giddiness if the psychological pre-conditions were lacking.

However, in this paper I wish to confine myself to some of the psychopathological aspects of his vertigo and to make some suggestions as to why unconsciously he wanted to feel giddy and what in his fantasy he thought he was doing by making everything rotate.

Vertigo is a sensation which occurs when one's sense of equilibrium is threatened. To an adult it is a sensation which is usually, though by no means always, associated with threats to the maintenance of the erect posture, and there is, therefore, a tendency to think of giddiness exclusively in terms of such relatively mature anxieties as the fear of falling over or the fear of heights and to forget that infants, long before they can stand, experience threats to their equilibrium and that some of their earliest activities such as grasping and clinging represent attempts to maintain the security of feeling supported by the mother. As the infant learns to crawl and later to walk the supporting function of the mother is increasingly taken over by the ground; this must be one of the main reasons why the earth is unconsciously thought of as the mother and why neurotic disturbances of equilibrium can so frequently be traced back to conflicts about dependence on the mother. Several analysts, e.g. Alice Balint (1933), Hermann (1936) and Schilder (1935) have discussed the way in which the infant's fear of being unsupported may become the prototype of later anxieties.

Vertigo is also closely related to the pleasure in motion which is usually discussed in the psycho-analytical literature under the heading of 'equilibrium erotism'. This differs from the closely related pleasure in movement (kinæsthetic and muscle erotism) in that an essential part of it is the sense of motion in relation to external objects. Abraham (1913) in his paper on Locomotor Anxiety distinguished between active and passive forms of this erotism, citing as examples the active pleasure of walking and the passive pleasure of travelling by train. Both forms readily become sexualized. French (1929), in a paper to which I owe much, reported a patient who developed vertigo as a transient symptom during analysis and who had rotating dreams. He interpreted the rotation in terms of the infant's pleasure in passive motion and particularly stressed the associated feeling of omnipotence. Although, as I hope to show, problems of passivity and omnipotence played an important part in my patient's psychology, I very much doubt whether the distinction between active and passive motion is either helpful or valid when applied to vertigo. As Schilder (1935) put it, vertigo is a 'borderline phenomenon' in which the boundary between subject and object becomes blurred and in which there can be confusion as to which is rotating. An experiment of Leiri's (1927), quoted by French, which I have repeated on myself, shows that important details of the actual sensation of vertigo can be altered by the attitude which the experiencing ego takes up towards it. If the ego takes up a passive attitude, the direction of rotation can be observed quite simply. Objects appear to be rotating either clockwise or anti-clockwise and there is no difficulty in deciding which. If, however, the vertigo is resisted and an attempt is made to fix some particular object, one immediately becomes confused. The fixed object appears to move in one direction and all objects behind it in the opposite. My patient, whose observations of his vertigo were, very naturally, never made in a spirit of scientific detachment, always maintained that everything spun round in both directions at once. This meant, I think, that he never took up a passive attitude towards his vertigo or allowed himself, as it were, to enjoy it. The conflict between the wish to feel giddy and the wish not to was actually represented in every attack. The same must have been true of French's patient, one of whose rotating dreams depicted a breast-shaped island moving in one direction while the background scenery moved in the opposite, and who only complained of vertigo during a period of active defence against passive wishes.

My patient was many years younger than his brother and three sisters and his upbringing was in many ways that of an only child. His mother was an ambitious and forceful character who combined an openly expressed regret that she was not a man with a contemptuous and depreciatory attitude towards the males of her own family. She very early decided that her youngest child would never do anything in life and that his only chance of realizing *her* ambitions was to marry money. If my patient's recollection is correct, she combined this psychologically castrating attitude with a sexual one, having been in the habit of kissing his penis and comparing it endearingly with a rosebud. His elder brother was, in some way that has never become clear, a disgrace to the family. He was, in fact, mentally ill all his life and after several periods in hospital committed suicide when in his middle fifties. One sister also committed suicide; the other two made marriages that did their mother credit. The father was a man apparently entirely without ambition who seemed content to be a rather unsuccessful traveller for a firm in which his wife's family had interests and who devoted much of his time to his hobbies of fishing and photography.

As a child and young man my patient took an especial pleasure in walking and running. As a boy he used to go for long country walks by himself, often stopping to masturbate. As a young man, during a phase in which his main interests were, as he now recognizes, unconsciously homosexual, he was a keen member of a cross-country running club. He has always been very proud of his ability to fall over without hurting himself and he once assured me that he could easily dive over the length of my couch without doing himself any damage. This claim, whether justified or not, suggests the presence of a counter-phobic attitude of the kind described by Fenichel (1939), which has been taken up as a means of mastering locomotor anxiety. Two other pieces of evidence, apart from the vertigo itself, point towards anxiety of this kind. During one phase of the analysis he had vivid, almost hallucinatory wishes that I should hold his hand, while he once dreamt that he was watching a small boy clinging to the side of a cliff. The boy's parents were standing by, doing nothing to help. The cliff was one that he often used to pass on a favourite cross-country run.

Compulsive masturbation began early. It was without conscious fantasy and gave little or no satisfaction. His earliest erotic sensations were experienced in association with a sliding game. He was, however, unsuccessful in attempts to introduce the pleasure of motion into masturbation. It proved, for instance, impossible to masturbate while riding a bicycle. Certain obsessive ruminations of his adolescence betray the same interest in motion. He speculated for years about possible methods of constructing a perpetual motion machine and was fascinated by the stars and planets. That these were disguised masturbation fantasies with an omnipotent content is suggested by the fact that he developed no particular interest in, or talent for, either physics or astronomy.

During much of his childhood he suffered from a painful and discharging left ear. In the early part of the analysis his recollection was that he had almost welcomed earache as affording an opportunity for being mothered, and it appeared that having drops put in his ear had been an enjoyable experience of a completely passive kind. This initial impression was incorrect. Originally he had hated it, but the necessity of submitting to his mother's ministrations had forced him to persuade himself that he enjoyed it. The sams defensive adoption of a passive attitude took place in respect of the insertion of suppositories for the relief of constipation. In many ways it epitomized his relation to his mother. That it involved eroticization of the ear is suggested by the fact that during his adolescence listening to the wireless with earphones on was a part of his masturbation ritual.

Although his mother had prejudged him a failure, it was his very success in proving her wrong that led to the events which precipitated his breakdown at the age of 45. Soon after her death, which occurred when he was 23, he became a travelling salesman for a small firm with which his family was connected. He soon showed exceptional energy and ability in salesmanship. Twenty years later he was rewarded for the part he had played in building up what had become a large and flourishing business by being made a director. Six weeks later he had his first attack of vertigo. From the time of his appointment until he started treatment with me a year later he was only occasionally fit for work since, in addition to the vertigo, various longstanding neurotic symptoms had increased in severity. These included headaches, compulsive masturbation, and a number of obsessional fears.

Although he was well aware that he was neurotic it never occurred to him that there could be any connexion between his Ménière's Disease and his other difficulties. There was one detail about it which put it right outside his previous experience and even prevented his realizing its similarity to the ordinary giddiness with which he, like everyone else, was familiar. This was the fact that the plane of rotation was at right angles to that of the giddiness which results from, for instance, over-enthusiastic waltzing. In order to reproduce the sensation he had it is necessary to bend one's head forwards 120 degrees while spinning, returning the head to its usual erect position as soon as one stops (Best and Taylor, 1939).

He had however noticed one fact which proved a valuable clue to the understanding of his vertigo. This was that attacks occurred only when he was elated. An interesting feature of these moods of elation was that they were always accompanied by the feeling that there was something spurious about them. Their association with vertigo was so regular that he learned to use them as a warning that an attack was probably imminent.

Treatment began, then, with my patient convinced that he suffered from a physical illness outside the scope of the analysis. My first hint of the possibility that his vertigo might become a part of the analysis was his reporting a number of dreams in which he was climbing, usually accompanied by a guide. One of them is worth quoting for the sake of its transparent symbolism. He had reached the top of a hill and was looking down onto the dome of St Paul's Cathedral. A woman turned to him and said 'There's no need to be frightened, you know'. I was nevertheless almost entirely unprepared when, in the twelfth week of analysis, he arrived at my consulting-room staggering, clutching at the furniture and holding to his mouth a towel into which he was vomiting. I helped him onto the couch and with great difficulty he told me what had happened. He had been at a meeting at which the sale of his business was being discussed. During the discussion he realized that very probably the sale would be made at a large profit and that his share of the proceeds might be sufficient to make him financially independent. He began to feel giddy and, as soon as the meeting was over, he announced his intention of resigning his directorship. Remembering his father's undistinguished career, I said I thought he felt guilty and anxious at the prospect of success that had been out of his father's reach, and that his panic-stricken resignation had been due to an unconscious fear of retribution. This interpretation met with no response. His physical condition was such that it seemed cruel and pointless to continue the session and I sent him home in a taxi. Next day he returned feeling much better and free from vertigo. I had, he said, been quite right the day before and he had withdrawn his resignation. I had certainly saved him thousands of pounds, he added. I was less satisfied; although my interpretation had apparently helped

19

him, and although it contained the implied symbolic interpretation of his vertigo that he felt he had climbed too high, it failed entirely to relate his attack to the general trend of the analysis up to that time.

The early weeks of the analysis had been largely devoted to elucidation of his sexual and marital difficulties. These were very complex and the details are beyond the scope of this paper. They arose out of the need to exclude from consciousness sadistic wishes ultimately directed at his mother and from attempts to force male genital activity into a passive mould.

There were, however, sessions during which the flow of verbal associations was replaced by violent physical activity. He would spend the greater part of these hours writhing on the couch, pulling his hair, burying his head in his hands and crying out for pity. This behaviour evoked in me images of a slave grovelling at the feet of a tyrannical master or a penitent abasing himself before a relentless deity. Interpretations based on these comparisons led to the discovery that in childhood he had a most literal belief in an omnipotent and implacable God, whose worldly representative was his mother. This belief had continued into adult life, long after his intellectual opinions had become those of a sceptic. The knowledge that he was still under the influence of this childhood fear brought him no relief. The reason for this was that these bouts of self-abasement were not transference-phenomena. They were part of a purely intrapsychic struggle between ego and superego in which the analyst as yet played no part.

The predominating transference-relationship at this time was characterized by the apparent paradox of great dependence coexisting with a complete absence of rapport. He doubted his capacity to manage without me over week-ends or during my holidays and entreated me to give him drugs. Yet neither he nor I had any feeling of being in touch with each other. This sense of a barrier between us was enhanced on his side by his feeling deaf, though in fact he had no difficulty in hearing me, and on my side by his habit of speaking in an almost inaudible voice. Despite these difficulties the analysis progressed, since he remembered my interpretations and worked on them himself between sessions. In this his behaviour was analogous to that of those animals who pouch their food and can only eat it when alone and free from danger.

The lack of rapport did not, of course, mean an absence of

transference. It was due to a defensive process. For instance, he made himself deaf, while his entreaties for drugs indicated a positive part-object transference. The need for his narcissistic withdrawal arose from the fact that the only (whole) object relationship he could envisage was one similar to that prevailing between his ego and superego.

The fear that I might be as cruel as his superego led him to conceive of me as the exact opposite of his mother. She had been a masculine woman whom, since he was the youngest of a large family, he had only known when middle-aged. So I was thought of as a young effeminate man, who had no recollection of any public event before about 1935 and who, if a momentary illusion or pseudo-hallucination of his could have been believed, doubled the profession of psycho-analyst with that of dancing in the male chorus of a musical comedy.

This illusion, like several others, which he had during the first few months of analysis, represented a wish to see me. As time went on the conflict between the wish to instate me as a good external object and the fear that to do so would involve the risk of finding out that I was as cruel as his superego grew more intense. In the ninth month of analysis he had to go out of London for two days in the middle of the week. Before going he denied any anxiety or annoyance at having to miss two sessions, but while away he had an attack of vertigo. On his return he dreamt that I had given him a bottle of Schnapps. The bottle was of a curious shape and had two different fluids in it. One of them was milk. He had been too embarrassed by the gift to thank me. His associations showed that the embarrassment referred to his inability to accept gifts or love, since to be beholden to anyone was to be at their mercy. It was this that made him unable to feel the dependence so clearly admitted in the dream, even though intellectually he saw quite clearly that no other interpretation was possible.

A fortnight later the situation changed suddenly. He had a 'blank' dream of the kind described by Lewin (1946, 1948) in his papers on the dream screen. It was accompanied by the feeling that I had taken him under my wing. Following Lewin, I interpreted this as representing the fulfilment in sleep of the wish for oral union with the analyst, who was being thought of as a breast, adding that he was accepting me as a helping, protecting figure instead of keeping me at a distance. My main reason for saying this was that for the first time I had a lively sense of rapport with him. My conviction that this could not be unilateral was confirmed by his saying at the end of the hour that he had suddenly realized that I was a human being. My justification for making an oral interpretation was not only material presented earlier in this paper, e.g. the dream in which I gave him a bottle of milk, but also the fact that for the last few months thumb-sucking and sleeping had been his major forms of self-consolation. (I have reported this dream in greater detail in Chapter 1 of the present volume).

It soon became clear that this dream had marked a turning-point in the analysis since after it all his symptoms seemed to have disappeared completely. Even immediately after the dream it was obvious that a great change had taken place, so much so that a superficial observer might have considered him cured. Two facts however showed that this was not so. One was that although his extra-analytical personal relationships improved remarkably, there was an apparent complete loss of libido; for the next six months he had no conscious sexual feelings of any kind. The other was that his very positive relationship with me was maintained by the use of the mechanisms of idealization and denial.

Both mechanisms were shown in a dream he reported three days later. It was the end of the month and the threat of my impending account led him to dream of Sir Stafford Cripps. His associations were concerned solely with the asceticism of Cripps' personal life; there was no mention of the fact that he was at that time (March 1950) Chancellor of the Exchequer. Similarly, although he missed his analysis when I took a fortnight's holiday, this did not imply any deprivation for him, since in his dreams he had completely satisfying analytical sessions.

As a result of his idealized positive transference and the feeling of omnipotence it gave him he was able to express hatred of his mother without any conscious guilt or anxiety. One night he dreamt that she lay dying. He was very pleased and had already inserted an 'advertisement' (*sic*) in *The Times* announcing her death. He assured his brother-in-law that she could not possibly last the night even though she was an 'unconscionable time a-dying'. Then he met a small boy, whom he did not tell about his mother's death, as he knew it would upset him too much. My suggestion that the small boy represented his own love for his mother was brushed aside, as was also my reminder that the king who apologized for being such an 'unconscionable time a-dying' bore the same Christian name as myself.

During this phase of the analysis it became clear that the twenty years of achievement and relatively good health that preceded his breakdown had been based on a system of dependence on idealized external objects, similar to though more complex than that which had now developed in the transference. In his own words, his self-esteem had always been 'borrowed' and 'Ersatz'. He had been an employee not an employer, had dealt with other people's money and goods not his own, and throughout the period he had had a very close alliance with an older man of quite exceptional drive. His car—it should be remembered that travellers spend much of their time driving —had also been a source of borrowed omnipotence; so much so that sometimes at night he had the alarming experience of feeling that he and it were expanding limitlessly, while other users of the road shrank to the size of midgets. When he became a director of the business, this system of dependence broke down completely. His passive, subtly sycophantic character, which had been one of his greatest assets as a salesman, became an insuperable handicap in a position that demanded decisiveness and a capacity to accept responsibility.

His dependence then and again in the transference brought with it attendant anxieties, which were due to the wish to incorporate the object he depended on. The manifest content of a dream depicted this clearly. First he was being chased by an old man who wished to rape him. He woke up in a panic, fell asleep again and dreamt he was driving to the Isle of Dogs. He saw me standing at the side of the road and gave me a lift, whereupon his car turned into a motor-cycle. A moment later he was carrying me on his back, and finally he was walking along with me imprisoned inside his testicles. The fear of homosexual rape portrayed in the first part of the dream was not only a defence against passive homosexual wishes; it was also fear of retaliation. If he wanted to steal and possess the analyst's potency, then according to the logic of the unconscious the analyst must want to do the same to him. A series of dreams about burglaries in which it was never quite clear whether he was the burglar or the burgled derived from the same anxiety.

Analysis of this system of 'borrowed potency' did not lead to a return of symptoms. In their place there emerged clearly the sadism which lay hidden behind his compulsive masturbation and which was the ultimate reason why psychic independence was impossible for him. This sadism centred round the specific fantasy of strangling a woman. Although this fantasy had many ramifications and spread over onto his relationship to his wife, making him fear that he might murder her, in the last resort it referred to his bad internal mother. The feeling was that only by squeezing all the life out of her and taking it into himself would he be able to live free of her domination. On one occasion—this was in the seventeenth month of analysis—he dramatized this fantasy very vividly on the couch, crying 'I've killed her. She's dead; and I loved her so dearly. Shall I ever be able to bring her back to life again?' The next night he dreamt that he met his mother and was surprised to discover that she was quite an ordinary person and not the ogress he had previously imagined her to be. This change of feeling about her remained with him after he awoke. During the following week he felt an increasing pressure in his abdomen as though something were growing inside it. Jokingly he suggested that he might be pregnant, in which case the baby would certainly be a monstrosity. More seriously he felt that it must be a mass of fæces. If only he could expel it with enough force and violence he would, he felt, be cured. Alternatively his tension would be relieved if he could have an attack of vertigo, though that, he knew, would not produce a lasting cure. However, his attempts to induce an attack were entirely unsuccessful. This fantasy of murdering and expelling his bad internal mother led in the transference to fears that his analysis would be brought to an abrupt end by my sudden death. He also had fantasies of strangling my children.

Much later, at the end of the third year of analysis, he again suffered from vertigo for a while, though the attacks differed from the earlier ones in several respects and were, I have little doubt, pure conversion symptoms. He was often giddy for hours without either feeling or being sick, while his general practitioner observed that these later attacks differed from the earlier ones in that his pulse was unaffected by them. My patient himself noticed that only objects on the periphery of his field of vision appeared to rotate. One is reminded of hysterical blindness which is often confined to the peripheral visual fields. In view of these differences I intend to ignore these later attacks, except to remark that on the couch they were sometimes accom-

panied by bodily movements which symbolized both the male
and female rôles in sexual intercourse.

In the preceding section I have tried to give a general
impression of the first ten months of his analysis during which
he had several attacks of vertigo, and to describe how this first
phase of the analysis came to a sudden end and was replaced
by a highly idealized positive transference which gave him
complete immunity from vertigo. I have suggested that this was
a transference-neurosis version of a defensive system that had
existed for the twenty years between his mother's death and his
appointment to a directorship.

This defensive system was clearly omnipotent in type and was
responsible for my patient being in some ways hypomanic. Its
instability, and, incidentally, its accessibility to therapy, arose
from the fact that an essential part of the defence was dependence on idealized *external* objects. Unlike the true (hypo-)
manic, whose sense of being at one with his superego makes him
pathologically independent of external objects, my patient
needed the support of idealized 'good' objects in the outer world
to compensate for his inner feeling of being disapproved of by
his superego. Since the most dangerous and threatening part of
his superego was an internalized phallic and castrating mother,
these external 'good' objects had to be either actually or sym-
bolically masculine. This was probably the most important
reason for his latent passive homosexuality.

His appointment to a directorship undermined these defences
in at least three different ways. In the first place it demanded of
him qualities that were incompatible with the passive sides of
his character. In the second, he could no longer 'borrow' his
potency from the business since he had become an intrinsic part
of it himself and, for instance, the other directors, on whom he
had previously relied, became his equals and, in a sense, rivals.
Thirdly, and most importantly, he felt unconsciously that by
taking up a position that required him to believe in his own
manhood he had defied his internalized phallic mother and had
been guilty of hubris in usurping her powers.

The failure of his omnipotent defences resulted in a state of
narcissistic withdrawal, with partial regression to an early oral,
schizoid position. He became incapable of maintaining whole
object relationships, consoled himself by thumb-sucking and

sleeping, both of which can be thought of as relationships with internal part-objects, and recaptured at moments the infant's capacity to hallucinate the object of its desire. In my previous paper I discussed in some detail the theoretical implications of his ability to hallucinate objects and simultaneously recognize them as illusions. Here I only wish to mention that it shows very clearly both the depth of his regression, which was to a stage before reality testing is firmly established, and the incompleteness of the regression, since part of his ego remained capable of testing reality and of contributing actively to the analysis. The split in his ego which this implies was *not* however my reason for describing the level to which he regressed as schizoid. I had in mind (*a*) the passive, sucking nature of his oral wishes, (*b*) the absence of any awareness of his own aggressiveness, and (*c*) his fear of all external objects. The anxiety he showed so clearly in his bouts of self-abasement had nothing to do with guilt about his own hostility or concern as to its effect on a loved object. It was terror at the imagined consequences of having dared to defy his internal mother. In Melanie Klein's terminology, it was paranoid anxiety; depressive anxiety and its accompanying wishes to restore the object destroyed in fantasy only came much later in the analysis when while dramatizing his strangling fantasies he cried 'I loved her so much. Shall I ever be able to bring her back to life again?'

Despite the absence of any conscious aggression during this first phase of the analysis three at least of his symptoms acted as outlets for the discharge of tension due to *un*conscious aggression. These were (*a*) his compulsive masturbation, (*b*) the bouts of self-abasement, and (*c*) the attacks of vertigo. That these last were aggressive in nature is shown by the facts that: (*a*) they ceased when he established a transference-relationship in which hostility was denied, (*b*) analysis of this transference-relationship led to the emergence of conscious sadistic fantasies, and (*c*) my patient himself equated his vertigo with anal expulsion of a bad internal object.

In interpreting his vertigo as a means of discharging aggressive tension due to an internal conflict between ego and super-ego, i.e. in economic terms, I have had in mind the fact that such an interpretation would be a tenable one even if the vertigo were an actual-neurotic[1] symptom, the form of which was

[1] Strictly speaking this is a misuse of the term 'actual neurosis' which properly refers to the somatic effects of tension due to damned-up libido.

determined entirely by the presence of inner ear disease and which was therefore without psychological meaning itself. If, on the other hand, it had psychological meaning and actually expressed an unconscious wish, that wish must have been, I think, to destroy his internal mother and to effect an almost complete dissolution of his internal object relationships by a 'black-out of rage', to use my patient's own phrase. A number of observations suggest that such an interpretation is correct, though it must be admitted that each taken singly is capable of an alternative explanation.

(1) One day early in the analysis he remarked that everything had been going round so fast that he wondered the house hadn't fallen down. The previous night he had dreamt that an engineer told him that almost the whole of his house would have to be pulled down before electricity could be installed. This dream expresses in very obvious symbolism the wish to 'pull down' his internal mother in order to achieve sexual potency and the psychological liberation that that implies.

(2) I have notes of several dreams in which other people were spinning round, but none in which he himself was. In every case the person spinning was either a female superego figure, e.g. a music mistress spinning round on a music-stool, or someone of whom he had good reason to be envious.

(3) The idea of a catastrophic explosion in which he and everybody and everything he depended on was destroyed exerted a great fascination over him and lay at the root of his obsessional fears. His private word for sexual intercourse was a 'bang'. The sadistic and anal implications of this are sufficiently obvious. I have already mentioned his spontaneous equation of vertigo with defæcation.

This brings me to my last point, which is, I suspect, a restatement of Schilder's remark that vertigo is a 'borderline phenomenon'. This is that my patient's vertigo was not only aggressive; it was sado-masochistic. The internalization of his mother and his oral dependence on her meant that his hostility towards his superego was self-destructive, since he felt that she was part of him and that, if she were killed, he must of necessity die too. It was only the fact that 'almost', i.e. not quite, 'the

The alternative concept of 'conversion' was not available since conversion symptoms have a psychological meaning. But cf. Schilder (1942), who speaks of 'vestibular irritation by conversion of sadistic impulses'. Cf. also Freud (1910).

whole' of his house had to be pulled down that prevented his vertigo being suicidal. Otherwise he would have been like Samson who, in avenging himself on the Philistines who had unmanned him, killed himself. The elation that preceded each attack of vertigo was analogous to Samson's final access of strength; it was the courage that comes of despair.

3

On Idealization, Illusion, and Catastrophic Disillusion[1]

Fairly soon after the beginning of her analysis a patient reported a dream in which the moon fell out of the sky into a dustbin. The night, however, remained bright as another moon was shining in its place. Her only comment on the dream was the rather sarcastic one that, of course, her previous psychotherapist would have said that the moon stood for either the breast or the vagina. In the absence of further associations, no interpretation was attempted and the dream was never referred to again. I shall return later to the significance of what was for this patient a characteristic piece of behaviour—giving me material which was tantalizing in its apparent significance, but doing so in such a way that I was unable to make any use of it.

I was reminded of this dream when, some months later, I was reading an English translation of some poems by Giacomo Leopardi, the Italian romantic poet of the early nineteenth century. One, an early fragment written when the poet was 21, describes a dream in which the moon falls out of the sky and burns itself out in a field. The dreamer then looks up at the sky and is frozen with terror at the sight of the hole from which the moon has been torn. I quote the poem in full. It is written in the form of a dialogue between the dreamer, Alcetas, and his companion, Melissus.[2]

[1] Paper read before the British Psycho-Analytical Society on 17 February 1954 and first published in the *Int. J. Psycho-Anal.* (1955), 36.
[2] *Poems from Giacomo Leopardi*, translated and introduced by John Heath-Stubbs (London: John Lehmann, 1946). Quoted by the kind permission of translator and publishers.

29

The Terror by Night
(A FRAGMENT)

ALCETAS: *Hear me, Melissus; I will tell you a dream*
I had last night, which comes to mind again,
Now that I see the moon. I stood at the window
Which looks out on the field, and turned my eyes
Up to the sky; and then, all of a sudden,
The moon was loosened; and it seemed to me
That coming nearer and nearer as it fell down,
The bigger it appeared, until it tumbled
In the middle of the field, with a crash, and was
As big as a water-pot; and it spewed forth
A cloud of sparks, which spluttered, just as loud
As when you put a live coal under water
Till it goes out. For it was in that way
The moon, I'm telling you, in the middle of the field,
Went out, and little by little it all turned black,
And round about the grass went up in smoke.
And then, looking up at the sky, I saw was left
A kind of glimmer, or mark, or rather a hole,
From which it had been torn, and at that sight
I froze with terror; and don't feel easy yet.

MELISSUS: *And well you might, indeed; for sure enough,*
The moon might tumble down into your field.

ALCETAS: *Who knows? For don't we often see in summer*
Stars falling?

MELISSUS: *But then, there are so many stars:*
And little harm if one or other of them
Do fall—there's thousands left. But there is only
This one moon in the sky, and nobody
Has ever seen it fall, except in dreams . . .

It will be seen that, unlike my patient's dream, Leopardi's was a nightmare. The reassurance my patient gave herself during sleep was only provided by Leopardi's waking consciousness, and even then it is attributed not to the dreamer but his audience. An interesting minor detail is that the dream only comes to mind again when the dreamer sees that the moon is, in fact, still in the sky.

Although, working along the rather direct lines apparently

practised by my patient's previous therapist, one can immediately suggest an interpretation in terms of castration anxiety and the primal scene, the poem's full emotional significance can only be appreciated in the light of imagery recurrently used by Leopardi. For him moonlight represented a state of illusion and the setting of the moon disillusion. This is stated explicitly in his last poem, 'The Setting of the Moon', which was written two hours before his death at the age of thirty-eight. In this poem, which is, unfortunately, too long to quote in full, the moon is described as creating 'a thousand images, illusory and fair' — 'a thousand sense-deceiving objects' in another translation — and its setting is used as a simile to describe the loss of hope which was for Leopardi the inevitable companion of growing old. 'Away depart the shadowy forms and beautiful illusions; less now seem those far-off hopes on which our suffering mortal nature learned to lean.' This poem in which the setting of the moon is used as a symbol for a gradual, life-long loss of hope, justifies us, I think, in interpreting the nightmare of nearly twenty years earlier as depicting the threat of a sudden, catastrophic disillusion, the collapse of a 'secondary construction' based on illusion and idealization which was maintained as a defence against a sense of despair and futility.

This point is well made in language proper to literary criticism by Leopardi's translator, John Heath-Stubbs, in that part of his introduction in which he discusses Leopardi's philosophy of life.

. . . Leopardi believed the normal condition, and the greatest evil, of human existence to be *noia* ('spleen' or tedium) and from this men sought to escape through various illusions of pleasure. . . . It is a purely negative state, antipathetic to the creative mood of the artist, so that every successful poem represents, in fact, a temporary escape from it. The loss of the ideals and illusions which make this escape possible is a continually recurring theme with Leopardi. . . . Lastly, we must remember Leopardi's intense feeling for the beauty of nature, closely linked as it is with these same themes. In particular he seems to be haunted by the image of landscape transfigured by moonlight, and the moon itself becomes for him a symbol of a transitory, though ideal beauty. In his early fragment, 'The Terror by Night' (an actual dream-poem), he envisages, perhaps, the condition of a world where this light has been suddenly extinguished; and in his latest poem, 'The Setting of the Moon', which was actually written on his death-bed, the same theme is handled for the last time.

That Leopardi's extreme pessimism sprang from a deep temperamental melancholy there can be no doubt, and his life offers many features which would interest a psycho-analyst. His relationships with women, though partly inhibited by the circumstances of his bodily deformity, give evidence of a certain abnormality, as well as a strongly developed capacity for passionate idealization. Ranieri states categorically that he never experienced the normal consummation of love. That the peculiar circumstances of his upbringing, and in particular his unhappy relations with his mother, played an important part in determining the course of his development, I have no doubt. I do not think it altogether fanciful to maintain that the feelings towards his mother may be connected with the development of his attitude to Nature. At first the beauty of Nature is dwelt upon in his poems, but Leopardi comes more and more to repudiate her, and to regard her as a force hostile to Man.

It is, actually, fairly certain that 'The Terror by Night' was written in what is generally recognized to have been Leopardi's most critical year, during which, by a process of sudden religious 'de-conversion', he lost his faith and replaced it by the pessimistic philosophy of life described in the previous quotation. Another poem of the same period. 'The Dream', describes 'the ghost of her by whom I first was taught what love is, and who later left me weeping'. For several months of this year he lived in a state of inertia in which he felt, as he said, 'like a living corpse' and suffered from a temporary blindness, which, like his deformity, is attributed by his biographers to overreading. A year earlier he had been overwhelmed by the discovery that he had 'a heart endowed with a capacity for loving so immense, that it despaired from the first of ever finding in this world an object adequate to its satisfaction'. This intuition of impotence followed his first infatuation with a female cousin, who was already married and a mother. (Unlike 'The Terror by Night', 'The Dream' is, presumably, not a genuine dream-poem, since it is a fairly close imitation of a poem by Petrarch. The facts and quotations in this and later paragraphs are taken from Bickersteth.[1])

[1] *The Poems of Leopardi*, translated and edited by Geoffrey L. Bickersteth. (Cambridge: University Press, 1923.)

Leopardi's impotence and the fact that he was the son of a dominating puritanical mother and an ineffectual though gifted father do, in fact, justify an interpretation of 'The Terror by Night' in terms of castration anxiety. A castrating, feminizing conception of sexual intercourse is surely depicted in the image of the moon crashing to the ground, spluttering like 'a live coal under water' and leaving in the sky 'a hole, from which it had been torn'. This interpretation can be reconciled with Leopardi's use of the moon as a symbol for illusion and ideal beauty if one assumes that the dream expresses an internal anxiety situation. The moon represents not the real, external penis but the idealized, internal penis of poetic creativeness which has been hypercathected as a means of overcoming the sense of despair engendered by recognition of his actual, sexual impotence. Theoretical considerations relating to the regressive effects of castration anxiety and the psychodynamics of the poetic impulse makes it certain that this idealized penis is also an internal breast.

It is, however, no part of my purpose to explore the hazardous reaches of psycho-analytical literary criticism. My only reason for turning to Leopardi's poetry is in the hope of illuminating the psychological problems of idealization and disillusion in general, and, as a particular instance, my patient's dream. If one assumes that for her, as for Leopardi, moonlight represented illusion and the moon the idealized object that maintains the state of illusion, one can interpret her dream in a way which is not only meaningful in itself but which also accords well with the pattern of her neurosis. The moon falling out of the sky represents the loss of an idealized good object. The fact that it falls into a dustbin represents denial of the value of the lost object and its sadistic, anal expulsion, while the second moon shining in the sky shows that the lost object, its loss denied, has been immediately replaced by another idealized object.

My patient was the younger daughter of neurotic and unhappily married parents who separated soon after her birth. Her introduction to life must have been not only frustrating but tantalizing, since her mother made unsuccessful attempts to overcome her anxiety about suckling her baby by being hypnotized. In her second year she suffered total separation from her mother for a period of over three months. Two of her earliest recorded remarks foreshadowed aspects of her later development. They were 'Why should I always have to be unhappy just because Mummy is?' and 'I love my sister [i.e. not her mother] better than anyone else in the whole world.' At least as early as the age of 4 she began the series of infatuations with older girls, teachers and female friends of her mother, which formed the pattern of her emotional life. These passionate attachments all bore the marks of idealization, the objects being unattainable and frustrating since they were chosen from outside her own family and age-group and were inevitably less interested in her than she was in them. The sadistic motive of making her mother feel unwanted was apparent in several of these attachments. This contributed to her unconscious fear of her mother, which was expressed in a fantasy of being pursued by a witch or ghost, who, as her analysis later showed, was felt to reside inside her own body.

Those who idealize their love-objects live in a fool's paradise, and my patient's infatuations necessarily tended to be short-lived. Either the object was indifferent, in which case the relationship became too humiliating to be tolerated, or, even worse, it was responsive, in which latter case the discrepancy between her emotional expectations and what the object could really give her led eventually to disillusion, anger, and bitterness. These feelings, however, never lasted long. A short period of hatred or despondency was soon followed by the instatement of a new ideal, the discovery of a new perfect object, who would be able to satisfy all her desires and rescue her from her unhappiness. Although one moon had fallen out of the sky and momentarily all was darkness, another one could always be put in its place. But the object she had discarded could not really be thrown away as easily as it was in her dream. She felt, she once told me, as though she had murdered all her lost objects.

During her analysis this pattern was inevitably repeated in the transference. She came to me precipitately from a non-Freudian psychotherapist in a state of severe, hysterical depression with several accompanying conversion symptoms. In the first hours she oscillated between daydreams of my taking her home with me and giving her tea with bread and honey — her night-dreams were more obviously erotic than this — and terrifying images of me in which I had large breasts that were crumbling to pieces. Later the frustrations of analysis led her to treat me as she had her mother. Since her analyst was a physician he had to be snubbed by her seeking her cure and salvation from osteopaths, homoeopaths, and nature-healers. Since his therapy was a 'talking-cure' involving no physical contact she had to try to overcome her sexual activities and invoke, unsuccessfully, the help of a gynæcologist in curing her frigidity. If any of these therapist mother-substitutes could be provoked into making disparaging remarks about psycho-analysis, so much the better. Telling me a dream in such a way as to arouse my interest and then by her comment on it challenge me to do better than her previous therapist, without in fact giving me any opportunity to do so, was part of the same pattern.

Although it was clear in this case that the mechanism of idealization was suborned to fulfil a sadistic purpose, it cannot, I think, be maintained that this is one of its primary functions. The purpose of idealization would seem rather to be to enable the ego (a) to deny feelings of hopelessness and emptiness which have arisen as a result of a withdrawal of cathexis from real, external objects, and (b) to evade the necessity of recognizing and resolving the ambivalence which would have to be faced if available, real, external objects were ever to be re-cathected. My patient had to idealize objects other than her mother since the only other alternatives were to lose all belief in life or to hate, and expect to be hated by, her mother or, in adult life, any other person from whom love might be attainable. Similarly, Leopardi's idealization of women is to be connected with the fact that, according to Bickersteth, he 'committed to his notebook one of the most terrible indictments ever penned by a son against his mother' even though 'he always treated her outwardly with the most scrupulous respect'.

It will be seen that I have attached central importance to withdrawal of cathexis from real, external objects as an insti-gator of idealization-processes. The initial tendency to with-drawal can be ascribed, according to one's theoretical predilec-tions, to one of three possible factors: (a) a frustrating discre-pancy between libidinal expectations and the amount of libi-dinal satisfaction actually experienced, (b) fear of the external object resulting from projection on to it of endogenous destruc-tive impulses, and (c) a failure on the part of the environment to arouse the infant's libidinal expectations and maintain them by

35

a modicum of satisfaction. (I shall return later to the significance of the distinction between the first and last of these three alternatives.) It will, however, be generally agreed that the tendency arises in the matrix of the infant's first emotional relationship with external reality, i.e. in its early relationship with its mother. There will, I think, be little doubt that in the material I have presented the obvious interpretation that the moon represents the breast is a correct one.

The close and complex inter-relationship existing between idealization on the one hand and withdrawal of cathexis from external reality on the other is illustrated by the fact that in everyday speech the word 'disillusion' is used to describe two psychological processes that at first sight seem to be psychopathologically quite distinct. It is used to denote not only loss of illusions, i.e. the discovery that things are not as one had incorrectly imagined and hoped them to be, but also loss of the ability to find value and interest in things as they actually are. Indeed, the latter is probably the commoner use of the word. In this paper I have so far used it in the first sense to describe the disenchantment that is the emotional hazard of those whose stability is based on the over-use of idealization. I could, however, equally well have used it to describe the initial disturbance in object-relationships that sets the tendency to idealization going. Although this ambiguity can be taken as an indication of the extent to which human beings rely on 'secondary constructions', it can also be seen as some confirmation of the idea which is so central to the thought of Winnicott (1945) and Milner (1952), the idea that an element of illusion enters into the realistic libidinal cathexis of external reality. If, as they maintain, illusion is an essential part of the cathexis of reality, then withdrawal of cathexis is, in an entirely uncynical sense, a process of disillusion.

This seeming paradox of supposing illusion to play an essential part in the cathexis of reality can be resolved, I believe, if one takes two considerations into account. The first is the obvious but easily forgotten one that the notion refers not to the individual's total relationship to reality but only to the erotic component of the total cathexis. It refers not to the purely nutritive 'ego-instinct' aspects of the infant's relationship to its earliest environment but only to those parts of it which are concerned, even if only nascently, with love.

The second consideration to be taken into account is that this

36

conception of the function of illusion can be taken as an extension and elaboration of one of Freud's earliest and most fundamental ideas. This is the idea that wishes tend towards hallucinatory self-fulfilment and that when the reality-sense is in abeyance, as in sleep, or has yet to be firmly established, as in infancy, cathexis of a hallucinated imago of the object leads to at least temporary satisfaction of the wish. This is, of course, not exactly the way that Freud himself put it. He wrote more in terms of hallucinatory gratification of wishes than in terms of hallucination of gratifying objects. But since he assumed that this involved regressive cathexis of memory-traces, one is justified, I think, in speaking of cathexis of a hallucinated imago. I shall return later to this point when I shall suggest that cathexis of this imago involves something more than a shift from perception to memory. Using this concept of a hallucinated imago, one can say, I think, as a first approximation that Winnicott and Milner have in mind the idea that the development of a healthy erotic relationship with reality involves that at the moment of consummation of a wish there should be a convergence and merging of this hallucinated imago (and its cathexis) with the imago of the available external object, not a shift of cathexis from one imago to the other. Failure to fuse these imagos leads to a divorce between the imaginative and intellectual functions that is, in principle at least, unnecessary. Successful fusion, on the other hand, leads to freedom from the belief that desire and reality are in inevitable opposition to one another and, in Milner's words, to 'the development of a creative relation to the world'. I think Milner would agree that this creative relation includes the capacity for ecstatic and joyful experience of external reality (i.e. ecstasy which is not based on manic defence). Absence of this ecstatic, creative element is probably often responsible for the sense of disappointment which seems so often to follow sexual intercourse even in individuals with apparently unimpaired orgastic capacity and which is so vividly expressed in the old Latin tag *'omne animal post coitum triste'*.

Disbelief in the possibility of finding joy in life and the associated divorce between intellect and imagination can be seen in Leopardi's view that illusions are a necessary escape from reality and his identification of Science with death and Poetry with life.[1] If translated into the language of psycho-pathology this implies the necessity for a transfer of cathexis from external

[4] Bickersteth, *op. cit.*, p. 8.

reality on to the hallucinatory imago and its imaginative elaborations. This shift of cathexis leads to the creation of ideal and
idealized internal objects, which are cathected at the expense of
external object-relationships. Re-projections of these internal
objects, like my patient's infatuations and Leopardi's belief in
his Muse, represent an attempt to recover the capacity for
object-relationships without having to deal with the difficulties
that arose in the original external object-relationship.

This way of stating the matter seems to imply the formation
of internal objects by a simple process of displacement of cathexis from one imago to another without involving introjection.
One can see, however, that this is not the case if one considers
the processes that underlie the primitive capacity for hallucinatory gratification. According to Freud it is based on the activation of memories of past satisfactions (and not on the presence
of any innate idea of an object from which satisfaction is expected and which is automatically cathected in states of instinctual tension). Since the hallucinatory gratification is presumed to be an experience of pure pleasure, this involves dissociation of the memories of past satisfaction from those of past
pain, even though the pain and pleasure will both have arisen
in relation to the same external object. One must add, therefore,
that splitting of introjected object-imagos (memories) into ideal
good and ideal bad imagos is also involved. In other words the
hallucinated imago is formed by a double process of introjection and splitting. This mode of formation explains why my
patient's compulsion to idealize was accompanied by the fantasy of a witch residing inside her own body and why Leopardi
as he grew older came to see in the nature he had previously
loved a force actively hostile to man.

The relationship of these processes to the problem of illusion
can only be understood if one realizes that they presuppose that
a certain primitive adaptation or response to reality has already
taken place. Freud's hypothesis that the infant in states of instinctual tension tends to hallucinate by cathecting memories of
past satisfactions assumes that it has already become capable
of having gratifying experiences and that its drives to seek satisfaction, i.e. to wish, have already been activated. That there is a
necessity for such an activation of instinct can be seen if one
turns to the work of, for instance, Ribble (1943) on 'stimulus
hunger', or the ethologists (Tinbergen and Lorenz) who, as
Bowlby (1952) has recently told us, have shown that innate

patterns of behaviour require the presence, at critical phases of their development, of certain 'sign' stimuli for their release. In the absence of these sign stimuli, potential patterns of behaviour never become manifest. It is Winnicott's contention, I believe, that early infancy is such a critical phase and that the importance of the early mother-infant relationship lies not only in the amount of satisfaction received by the infant but also in the degree of correspondence between the infant's latent impulses, wishes, or needs and the mother's provision of the kind of stimuli necessary for their release. Insofar as the mother arouses the infant's libidinal expectations and maintains them by a modicum of satisfaction, its perception and conception of reality will accord with the pattern of its inherent instinctive tendencies, and impulses will not merely tend to be directed towards an external reality which is subjectively felt to be good but will actually be developmentally bound to the imagos of the reality that has released them. An imaginative sense of reality will develop which is stable because its development is part of the infant's relf-realization.

Subjectively, that is, from the infant's point of view, to the extent that external reality has played into its unconscious expectations, it will develop the illusion, as Winnicott puts it, that it has created its objects, or, to put it the other way round, will be spared for a while the awareness that its objects are not part of itself, have not been created omnipotently by its own desires. Though this illusion will require an eventual disillusion, the disillusionment will be confined to its belief in its omnipotent control of reality, not to reality itself. The healthy child's hero-worship of its parents and its belief in their omnipotence is to be seen as a normal process of idealization which tides it over this period of disillusion until such time as it can rely on its own powers and discovers itself as an individual, potent but not omnipotent.

If, however, the environment fails to maintain a modicum of satisfaction, impulses, to the extent that they have arisen at all in a frustrating environment, will lack firm attachment to the imagos of real, external objects and external reality will be subjectively felt as tantalizing and bad. The path to external reality not being firmly established, impulses will tend to be directed inwards and will attach themselves to the only other available imagos, the ideal objects created by splitting of introjected object-imagos. These ideal internal objects will certainly be present, to some extent at least, for the simple reason that psycho-analysis only has cognizance of living infants. Those that receive no stimulation, no gratification, die.

The infant's illusion that it has created its objects, its imagination, and, indeed, its sense of reality, for it will in a way have created its objects, will refer not to external reality but to ideal, internal objects, and the stage will be set for the development of pathological idealization-processes of the kind described in the clinical material I have presented.

SUMMARY

The first of the two notes is an analysis of two very similar dreams, one reported by a patient, the other recorded in a poem by Giacomo Leopardi (1798–1837). The central theme of both is the moon falling out of the sky. Material, clinical in one case, literary and biographical in the other, is presented to show that in each the moon represented an idealized internal object and its falling out of the sky disillusionment and the collapse of a defensive 'secondary construction', based on illusion and idealization. The relationship of the anxiety inherent in both dreams to castration anxiety is discussed.

The material presented in the first note is used to provide illustrative examples for the second, which considers the relationship between pathological idealization, with its attendant risk of pathological disillusion, and illusion and disillusion as normal processes playing an essential part in the establishment of external object relations and 'the development of a creative relation to the world' (Winnicott and Milner). It is suggested that:

(*a*) Pathological idealization is the result of a defensive hypercathexis of imagos produced by splitting of introjected external object imagos and their later imaginative elaboration.

(*b*) That this hypercathexis is the result of a quantitatively significant lack of correspondence between the infant's latent impulses and the stimulation and satisfaction provided by the environment.

(*c*) That, conversely, to the extent that there is correspondence, the infant feels that external reality has 'played into' its unconscious expectations and acquires the illusion that it has created its objects omnipotently. The later 'normal' disillusion will be confined to its belief in its omnipotence.

ILLUSION AND DISILLUSION

(*d*) That in cases such as those described in the first note, this illusion of creativity becomes attached to ideal internal objects, leading to pathological states of illusion and idealization with their ever-present risk of catastrophic disillusion.

4

Symbolism and its Relationship to the Primary and Secondary Processes[1]

The purpose of this paper is to discuss the relationship of symbolic processes to ego-functioning. I have started by restating Freud's initial formulation of the differences between the primary and secondary processes with special reference to Winnicott and Milner's concept of illusion (Section I). I have then gone on to suggest reasons why, in my opinion, it is not only misleading to restrict, as some writers do, the concept of symbolism to the use of symbols by the primary process, but also incompatible with Freud's later views on the nature and development of the ego (Section II). In this section I have been much influenced by Milner and Kubie, both of whom have written in favour of an extension of the classical analytical concept of symbolism. In the third and last section I have attempted to reformulate the theory of symbolism on the basis of the assumption that symbolization is a general capacity of the mind which is based on perception and which may be used either by the primary or the secondary process. My immense debt to Jones's classic paper 'The Theory of Symbolism' (1916) will be obvious throughout, even when I take up a position diverging from his.

I have also been profoundly influenced by Brierley's conception of metapsychology as process-theory and her stress on the need to relate psycho-analytical theory to the trend of modern thought which is 'a movement away from analysing into things and towards analysing into processes' (Waddington, quoted by Brierley, 1951). One implication of this stand-point is that dynamic and economic formulations in terms of process and organization are, when possible, to be preferred to topographical descriptions, which tend to be static and to encourage reification, i.e. the fallacy of forgetting that concepts such as ego and id are fictions and endowing them with a concrete

[1] A slightly longer version of this paper appeared in the *Int. J. Psycho-Anal.* (1956), **37**.

reality only possessed by such 'things' as, for instance, bodily organs. This is the reason for my having on occasion restated familiar notions in unfamiliar terms.

I

The distinction between primary and secondary processes was one of Freud's earliest and most fundamental ideas. He founded his metapsychology on the assumption of a primitive psychic apparatus, the activities of which are directed by an attempt to regulate states of tension by discharging instinctual impulses. This psychic apparatus is patterned on a reflex arc, the sensory side of which carries endogenous impulses of somatic origin, the motor side of which discharges these impulses, thereby abolishing the tension to which they tend to give rise. He further assumed that there are on the motor side two psychic modes and pathways of discharge. These two modes of discharge he called the primary and secondary processes.

If an impulse is discharged by way of the primary process, the end-result is either a waking or sleeping hallucination. If the latter, it is what we call a dream. The mechanism by which this occurs is that the energy or libido carried by the impulse passes, not towards those bodily organs which might effect a real satisfaction of the impulse, but towards that part of the psychic apparatus in which memories of past satisfactions are represented. The memory-traces or imagos of the objects which provided these past real satisfactions are thus invested with energy (cathected) and experienced as real. The memory-imago is converted into a hallucination by precisely the same process that in normal waking life makes any part of the external world subjectively real, by being invested with libido. The fact that a symbol may be substituted for the memory-imago will be considered in Section III.

The pre-condition of memory-imagos and symbols being converted into hallucinations in this way is withdrawal of cathexis from external reality and functional immobilization of those parts of the mind that are orientated towards external reality. This occurs under at least four different conditions:

(*a*) Sleep, hence dreams.
(*b*) Psychosis in which there is a defensive denial of reality.

Freud was much impressed by the existence of simple wish-fulfilling hallucinoses, which were first described by one of his teachers in neuro-psychiatry, Meynert. The fact that the great majority of psychotic hallucinations have a much more complex psycho-pathology does not, of course, invalidate the importance of this observation.

(c) Infancy, in which immaturity of the ego facilitates hallucinatory wish-fulfilment. It was, I think, Freud's view that all infantile impulses are at first dealt with by hallucination and that only when the tension passes beyond a certain critical point is pain experienced.

(d) Neurosis, in which partial withdrawal of interest from the outer world is accompanied by introversion and the development of a fantasy life based on a psychical elaboration of childhood and infantile memories.

In none of these four instances is the mind entirely under the infiuence of the primary process. In sleep the withdrawal of interest from the outside world is not so great as to prevent the sleeper registering significant external stimuli, e.g. signs of real danger, even though there may be an attempt to misinterpret them in such a way as to make it unnecessary to wake up. Similarly with dreams provoked by a full bladder or rectum: the dreamer usually wakes up in time. Nor is the infant entirely under the sway of the primary process; he has certain innate responses which are primitive adaptive activities, e.g. startle reaction, crying when not firmly supported and when hungry, etc.

In describing the course of an impulse when it is subjected to the primary process, I have by implication also described the secondary process. It is the process by which an impulse passes to that part of the psychic apparatus which (a) perceives external reality, and (b) controls those physical organs which can effect changes in the outside world which will lead to satisfaction of the wish (discharge of the impulse). That is to say, the secondary process is that process by which an impulse becomes a more or less conscious wish, which is satisfied, not immediately by hallucination, but only after a delay during which (a) external reality is perceived and analysed in the search for an appropriate object, and (b) skills of a more or less complex kind are used in such a way that the wish is satisfied. These skills may be either innate or acquired. In other words, the secondary process involves use of the functions of reality-testing and reality-manipulation. According to the particular conditions prevailing the secondary process may be more or less complex and involve more or less delay in discharge of the impulse.

The essential distinction between the primary and secondary processes can be conveniently expressed in two different ways, one of which stresses the fate of the impulse, the other the quality of the relationship to the object. According to the former the difference is that the primary process relieves tension immediately and independently of external reality but only temporarily, while the secondary process involves a delay, is dependent on reality but relieves tension permanently—permanently, that is, in respect of the impulse operating at any particular moment. It does not, of course, abolish the inherent tendency of impulses to recur. It is this difference between the two processes that explains the limited value of dreams. Unsatisfied wishes which would otherwise disturb sleep can be relieved immediately and completely by dreaming—*vide* Freud's dictum that the function of dreams is to preserve sleep—but no amount of dreaming will ever really and permanently satisfy the wishes; hence the eventual need to awaken and recathect external objects. Similar considerations explain the temporary success but ultimate failure of day-dreams and neurotic symptoms to give satisfaction.

In respect of the quality of the relationship to the object the essential difference is that the primary process is objectively autistic, this notwithstanding the subjective presence of an (internal) object-imago, whereas the secondary process leads to communication, contact and interaction with an external object, which, at the moment of consummation, is both objectively and subjectively present. The fundamentally autistic nature of the primary process is obvious in its simpler manifestations, but it tends to become obscured in its more complex elaborations. Following the use of projective and introjective identifications objects in the outside world may be treated, with or without their connivance, as unconscious substitutes for ideal, internal imagos. When this happens, a pseudo-object relationship develops which is technically psychotic[1] and potentially unstable, even though it may be (apparently) ego-syntonic

---

[1] Throughout this paper I have used the word 'psychotic' to refer to a particular quality or intensity of cathexis with which an internal object-imago may be invested. This cathexis, which arises from the primary process, gives the object-imago delusional or hallucinatory

45

and last a lifetime. Examples of this are *folie à deux*, perverse relationships and certain ideological groups.

It is important to realize that the primary and secondary processes are not clinically observable phenomena but theoretical constructs designed to explain a particular range of facts. They were designed to explain, in the first instance, neurotic and particularly hysterical introversion and fantasy and then, secondarily, dreams, in which Freud found a normal analogue of hysterical fantasy. The simplest possible formulation of the resemblance between neurosis and dreaming is that both are permeated by the primary process, by attempts to satisfy wishes not realistically by relationships with appropriate external objects but in an illusory manner by cathexis of internal object-imagos (cf. Jones, 1911).

Formulations of the difference between the primary and secondary processes tend to assume an antithesis between fantasy and reality, between imagined ideas of objects and real external objects. It is therefore important to realize that this antithesis is not always a valid one and that, as Winnicott (1945) has pointed out, conditions occur in which the distinction breaks down. The reason for this is that the satisfaction of certain wishes, e.g. those produced by oral and genital impulses, requires an object motivated by a reciprocal wish. Thus, for instance, satisfaction of an infant's oral wishes requires the active participation of a mother who wishes to suckle her baby. It may obviously happen that, as a result of the mother's actions, no appreciable or significant time elapses between the emergence of the infant's wish to be fed and the actual feed, i.e. that the breast appears before the baby has begun to suffer a painful degree of tension. (I am not assuming here that the mother satisfies the infant's wish to be fed the moment that the wish emerges—it is difficult even to conceive of a wish of this kind emerging at a particular moment in time—but that there is a period of time during which the wish is active without the infant entertaining any expectation that it will not be satisfied, and during which, therefore, the infant has no motive either to perceive or to deny external reality.) When this happens, what is the infant's subjective experience of the event? Is its perception

---

qualities, either actually if the imago is projected or potentially if it remains unprojected. Later in the paper I refer to such object-imagos as 'phantoms'.

of the real breast different in some way from the image of the breast which it hallucinates while under the influence of the primary process, or are the perceived and imagined breasts identical? If the latter, then we have a situation in which a real satisfaction occurs while the infant is under the influence of the primary process, in which a real experience is subjectively a hallucination. Repeated experience of this overlap or convergence of illusion and reality will tend to attach the individual positively to external reality without disturbances arising from denial, hatred, suspicion, disillusion, or withdrawal Although frustration may lead to acceptance of reality, only satisfaction can lead to love of it.

It is possible that the function of courting and fore-pleasure activity in adult sexual life is to produce an analogous state of affairs, in which the presence in both partners of synchronized reciprocal wishes leads to the abolition at the moment of orgasm of any distinction between fantasy and reality. If so this would explain the apparent paradox that the climax of object-love is a feeling of identification with the object or, as Fenichel puts it, that 'at the height of full genital satisfaction identification comes back at a higher level' (Fenichel, 1945, p. 85).

II

In the preceding section I have used the term 'primary process' in its restricted sense of the tendency to hallucinatory wish-fulfilment and have not adopted the wider usage, which includes in the concept all those features which Freud described as characteristic of the unconscious, i.e. symbolization, displacement, condensation, mobility of cathexes, absence of the categories of space and time, etc. I have done this for two reasons. First, certain of these features, mobility of cathexes, absence of the categories of space and time, and possibly, condensation, are logically necessary consequences of the tendency to hallucinatory wish-fulfilment and therefore do not call for special consideration. Secondly, inclusion of others, e.g. symbolization and displacement, in the concept of the primary process implies two things that are, I believe, untrue:

(i) That the modes of unconscious and conscious mental activity are qualitatively absolutely different, and, in particular,

(ii) that symbolization is a feature of unconscious mental activity and does not occur in conscious thinking.

47

The idea that unconscious and conscious mental activity are qualitatively different can, I think, be rejected on general grounds, since it ignores the fact that the mind, notwithstanding its propensity to conflict, dissociation, etc., is nevertheless a unitary structure which acts as a whole. It is therefore illogical to conceive of the mind as being subdivided into two subsidiary structures, an unconscious and conscious, or an ego and id, functioning in entirely different ways. Biologically speaking, one can only think in terms of one, the ego, being a specialized differentiation of the other, in the same way as—and this is probably more than an analogy—the cerebral cortex is a specialized differentiation of more primitive parts of the central nervous system. The fact that some aspects of cortical activity are sometimes conscious does not justify us in assuming that the cortex functions in a way basically different from the rest of the central nervous system.

The notion that symbolism is confined to unconscious mental activity is open not only to the general objection raised in the last paragraph but also to more specific ones. Firstly, it makes it very difficult to describe the process of sublimation and, in particular, to differentiate stable and progressive sublimations from neurotic and defensive (pseudo-) sublimations. Secondly, it is impossible to explain the nature of the therapeutic action of psycho-analysis without recognizing that the analyst, the analytical situation, and the words used in analytical treatment are all symbols. Thirdly, it runs counter to the clinical observation, which Freud made very early on, that there are individuals who possess spontaneous understanding of symbolic equations and who offer no resistance to interpretations of sexual symbolism. These individuals are not necessarily schizophrenics, as Freud at first thought. Nor incidentally are they always artists.

The difficulties involved in trying to restrict the concept of symbolism can be seen if one considers Jones's paper 'The Theory of Symbolism', which was written in 1916, i.e. before the development of ego-psychology. Here Jones maintains that there is such a thing as 'true' symbolism which can be differentiated from what he calls 'symbolism in its widest sense'—not, it will be noted, 'false' symbolism. On the one hand he writes 'If the word symbolism is taken in its widest sense, the subject is seen to comprise almost the whole development of civilization. For what is this other than a never-ending series of evolutionary

48

substitutions, a ceaseless replacement of one idea, interest, capacity, or tendency by another?' On the other hand he says 'symbolism arises as the result of intrapsychical conflict between the repressing tendencies and the repressed' and 'only what is repressed is symbolized; only what is repressed needs to be symbolized'. Further, in formulating the essential difference between 'true' symbolism and 'symbolism in its widest sense' he writes:

> The two cardinal characteristics of symbolism in this strict sense are (1) that the process is completely unconscious . . . and (2) that the affect investing the symbolized idea has not, insofar as the symbolism is concerned, proved capable of that modification in quality denoted by the term 'sublimation'.

This quotation shows that Jones has not just made an arbitrary and purely verbal distinction by restricting the concept symbolism to identifications between ideas, one of which is repressed and unconscious, but is making a real and very important distinction, viz. that between symbols that have become subordinated to the neurotic process and those that have been utilized in ego-development. There are, however, two interrelated objections to the way in which Jones has formulated this distinction.

The first is that it is surely more logical to say that symbolism is a general capacity which may be used in two different ways than to subdivide symbolism into two separate categories according to the two different uses to which it is put. The second is that the distinction used by Jones as a criterion to differentiate his two kinds of symbolism, i.e. whether the affect investing a symbol has or has not undergone 'that modification in quality denoted by the term "sublimation" ', is really a distinction between two kinds of affect, modified and unmodified, not one between two different kinds of symbol. The question whether one can, in fact, distinguish between different kinds of affect is not, I think, directly relevant to the theme of the present paper.

It will, I hope, be understood that the preceding paragraphs are not, in the ordinary sense of the word, a criticism of Jones's paper. They are rather a re-statement of some of the difficulties created by the immaturity of psycho-analytical theory at the time the paper was written, difficulties which must have played

49

their part in leading Freud to replace his earlier metapsychology by that of the 'Ego and the Id', in which (*a*) what is unconscious is not necessarily repressed, (*b*) the ego (replacing the conscious) is not necessarily conscious, and (*c*) the concept of a conscious opposing an unconscious is replaced by that of an ego which is 'that part of the id which has been modified by the direct influence of the external world'. It is this last which, in my opinion, makes the classical theory of symbolism untenable. The only justification for this present communication is my belief that analysts in their thinking about symbolism have not always fully appreciated the implications of ego-psychology and have tended to think of symbolism and ego-functioning as being two entirely unrelated fields of psycho-analytical study.

Two notable exceptions are Melanie Klein's paper on Symbol-Formation (1930) and Susan Isaacs's on Phantasy (1948). However, as should already have been obvious, I have adopted throughout this paper a standpoint diverging in several respects from Kleinian theory. One aspect of this divergence is perhaps worth discussing in some detail, since it bears directly on my main theme. This is in connexion with the concept of fantasy. On the only occasion that I have so far used this word I used it as an antithesis to external reality and not in its extended Kleinian sense of the 'unconscious mental content' underlying all behaviour, including both neurotic and realistic mental activity. This extension of meaning, which has, as I shall mention later, highly respectable literary precedents, seem to me to be at one and the same time extremely helpful and most misleading. Its value, I think, is that it draws attention to the fact that unconscious symbolic and imaginative processes underlie the development and maintenance of a sense of reality just as much as they do neurosis.

This is, of course, the main theme of this present paper. Its weakness in my view is that it tends to blur a distinction that was abundantly clear in classical analytical theory. This is the distinction between mental processes involving defensively-cathected, ideal, illusory 'psychotic' imagos—to which the term 'phantoms' might justly be applied—and those involving imagos based directly on memories of real experiences. This seems to me to be a fundamental distinction notwithstanding the fact that the former arise by idealization from the latter. The emphasis placed in Kleinian theory on the fact that 'psychical reality' and 'external reality' are both subjectively real does, I think, tend to obscure the fact that there are none the less essential differences between them, and that psychical reality is itself divisible into one part which is developmentally bound to external reality and another which has been formed by idealization (see Chapter 3 of the present volume.) The essential difference between 'external reality' and this second part of 'psychical reality' is, of course, that satisfactions provided by the former are objectively real while those provided by the latter are illusory and sense-deceiving. One sometimes gets the impression that in their quite justified reaction against a tendency to undervaluation of psychical reality some Kleinian analysts fall unwittingly into the opposite error of disparaging external reality. The fallacy of thinking of fantasy as *mere* fantasy, as Susan Isaacs put it, tends to be replaced by that of thinking of external reality as *mere* external reality. Another aspect of this blurring of distinctions is the tendency to proceed from the perfectly correct observation that all perception is unconsciously conceived af as a 'taking in' to an unjustified implied equation between perception and 'psychotic' introjection (and between recognition and 'psychotic' projection).

The need to reinstate the distinction classically maintained by the antithesis between fantasy and reality has, I think, been one of the reasons why Winnicott and Milner have introduced the concept of illusion. That this is in effect the reintroduction of an earlier concept has however been obscured by the fact that both have been primarily interested in defining the nature of the relationship between (the capacity for) illusion and (the perception of external) reality during the period of maximal reciprocity between the infant and its mother and in describing the way in which disturbances in this relationship lead to a divorce between illusion and reality. They have tended to take for granted the later vicissitudes of the conflict between illusion and reality after the split has occurred. These vicissitudes form the subject matter of classical psychopathology, in which the opposition between fantasy and reality is, within its limits quite correctly, taken for granted.

An additional help in reintroducing the classical distinction between fantasy and reality into the framework of a theory which no longer holds the distinction to be absolute, would be to use the word 'imagination' for the process of elaboration, organization, and configuration of imagos which subserves the secondary process and to restrict the term fantasy to the use of imagos by the primary process. This would have at least three advantages:

(*a*) It would enable the distinction between the primary and secondary processes to be clearly made without ignoring the fact that all reality-thinking is 'supported by unconscious fantasy', to use a phrase of Susan Isaacs's.

(*b*) It would be in accordance with common educated parlance, which recognizes that imagination is an essential prerequisite for a full appreciation of reality and that people can suffer from a lack of imagination.

(*c*) It would make available three words—illusion, fantasy and imagination—to cover the wide range of meanings previously embraced by fantasy. (At present the word is used to mean (i) a general mental activity, (ii) a particular, neurotic form of this activity, (iii) a state of mind arising from it, and (iv) the fictive realm in which it occurs.)

In this context the spelling of the word *phantasy* is of interest. According to Susan Isaacs the English translators of Freud 'adopted a special spelling of the word *phantasy*' to differentiate the psycho-analytical meaning of the term from the popular word *fantasy* meaning 'day-dreams, fictions and so on'. However, *fantasy* and *phantasy* have, according to the *Oxford English Dictionary* (1901), tended since the rediscovery of Greek learning to be 'apprehended as separate words, the predominant sense of the former being "caprice, whim, fanciful invention" while that of the latter is "imagination, visionary notion" '. In other words there has been a tendency to recognize that the notion of fantasy subsumes two different ideas, or alternatively that it is a process that may lead to two very different end-results. The clearest pre-analytical insight into the nature of fantasy would seem to have been that of Coleridge, who based his theory of Imagination (Fantasy) on a distinction between primary imagination, which he called 'the living power and prime agent of all human perception' and fancy, which he described as 'a mode of memory emancipated from the order of time and space', a phrase which almost sounds like a definition of the primary process. Unfortunately Coleridge's theories are so entangled with his idealist philosophy that they are probably of no practical use to psycho-analysts. I should however like to give two further quotations which suggest that he was dealing with the problem being discussed here and that the relevance is not merely apparent. These are (*a*) his concept of secondary imagination which is 'an echo of the former (i.e. primary imagination), co-existing with the conscious will, yet still identical with the primary in the *kind* of its agency, and differing only in *degree*, and in the mode of its operation. It dissolves, diffuses, dissipates (i.e. analyses) in order to recreate' (*Biographia Literaria*, 1817), and (*b*) his statement of the relation between Imagination and Fancy. 'Imagination must have fancy, in fact the higher intellectual powers can only act through a corresponding energy of the lower' (*Table Talk*, 1833) (I. A. Richards: *Coleridge on Imagination*, 1934).

III

In this last section, I shall try to formulate the theory of symbolism on the basis that symbolization is a general tendency or capacity of the mind, one which may be used by the primary or the secondary process, neurotically or realistically, for defence or self-expression, to maintain fixation or to promote growth. For the sake of brevity my formulation takes the form of fourteen propositions.

1. The process of symbol-formation consists in the displacement of cathexis from the idea of an object or activity of primary instinctual interest on to the idea of an object of less instinctual interest. The latter then operates as a symbol for the former.

This definition of symbol-formation requires expansion and clarification in two respects.

A. The notion of an object of primary instinctual interest is intended to include (*a*) the external object of a primary drive, (*b*) the parts of the self that are necessary for the establishment, maintenance, and consummation of a relationship with an external object, and (*c*) the substance that passes between subject and object.

B. I have used the phrase 'object or activity' in preference to just 'object' to draw attention to the fact that objects derive their significance from their function and that therefore the displacement in symbol-formation is from one process or function to another and not from one 'thing' to another. In what follows the word 'object' should be taken to mean 'function of an object'.

2. The object or activity onto which cathexis is displaced is one which the mind by its intrinsic organization is capable of associating with the primary object or activity. A symbol may

(*a*) resemble the primary object in appearance, function, or capacity to arouse an identical affect, or (*b*) be part of the primary object, or (*c*) have been experienced in spatial or temporal contiguity with it. These three kinds of relationship between the symbol and the symbolized correspond to the three figures of speech, simile, synecdoche, and metonymy (see Sharpe, *Dream Analysis*, Chap. 1).

3. A symbol carries affect displaced from the object it represents. In any particular instance the affect attaching to an object will be loving, hating, fearful, etc., and the symbol representing the object will be chosen on account of its aptness to carry that affect. The phallic symbols, dagger, watering-can, gun, aeroplane and snake—to use examples cited by Freud— all refer to different affective conceptions of the penis, and to different aspects of its functions.

4. The process of displacement from one object or activity to another is capable of indefinite repetition, so that schematically one can construct a series of symbolic equations, A the primary object or activity being symbolized by B, B by C, C by D, etc., each successive member of the series being more remote from, and having less intrinsic resemblance to, or connexion with, the primary object. In other words symbolism is a centrifugal, one-way process. Displacement of cathexis in the opposite, centripetal direction can however occur, and is characteristic of mental dysfunction arising from neurotic regression, cerebral damage, sleep, or fatigue. This centripetal displacement of cathexis is usually called 'regression', though it could as appropriately, and perhaps less confusingly, be called 'desymbolization'. One example of this, the replacement of word-images by visual images in dreams and states of fatigue, formed the basis of Silberer's theory of functional symbolism. According to the view expressed here, regressive visualization is the reverse of symbolization, not a special form of it. I shall return later to the symbolic nature of words.

5. The fact that an object or activity is itself of primary instinctual interest is no bar to its being used as a symbol. A penis may, and often does, represent a breast, or a head a penis. In such cases the object has a double cathexis, only one of which is capable of interpretation, the other being intrinsic and irreducible.

6. The process of symbol-formation presupposes some degree of ego-development, since the symbol-to-be has to be per-

ceived before it can be used as a symbol. Although there seems to be no objection to assuming that the mind possesses some kind of innate idea of the objects necessary for the satisfaction of its primary instincts (and also, presumably, of the 'sign stimuli' necessary for the release of instinctual drives and recognition of their objects) (cf. Tinbergen, 1953), the notion that symbols are innate implies either the inheritance of acquired knowledge or a collective unconscious. The so-called universality of symbols is better explained by reference to (a) 'the uniformity of the fundamental and perennial interests of mankind', to use Jones's phrase, (b) the uniformity of the affects and sensations accompanying instinctual acts (see Sharpe, 1940, on Metaphor), and (c) the uniformity of the human mind's capacity for forming Gestalts and seeing resemblances between them. This last is a fact that analysts can take for granted, since analyst and patient have minds that in this respect function in an identical way. This is why symbolic equations are perceived so easily so long as there is no emotional resistance operating. Things would be perhaps very different if inter-species analyses were attempted.

(The statement that symbolism is inherited can be found in contemporary analytical literature (e.g. Fliess, 1953). It seems to be based on a confusion of thought, since it is not made clear whether the word 'symbolism' means 'propensity to form and use symbols' or 'mode of acquiring symbols'. If the former, the statement is true but of no especial significance, since all propensities are presumably in some sense inherited. If the latter, the statement is untrue since either (a) it implies that acquired knowledge can be inherited, i.e. it is Lamarckian, or (b) it is self-contradictory, since the essence of a symbol is that it acquires its significance by displacement from something else, while the essence of an inherited idea is that its significance is intrinsic. If psycho-analytical symbols were inherited, this would, of course, provide a basis for making an absolute distinction between them and other kinds of symbols. In the Tenth Introductory Lecture (1916), where Freud describes symbolism as an 'ancient but obsolete mode of expression', he includes aeroplanes and zeppelins in his list of typical phallic symbols, an inclusion which is only compatible with Jones's view that each individual re-creates his symbolism anew by perception.)

7. Once a symbol has been formed it may be used either by the primary or the secondary process.

8. If used by the primary process the symbol is treated in exactly the same way as is the memory-imago of the primary object, for which it becomes an interchangeable substitute and representative. This is another way of putting Freud's statement that the primary process is characterized by mobility of cathexis. Further elaboration of this is unnecessary, since it would amount to a repetition, *mutatis mutandis*, of Section I. The simplest example of the utilization of a symbol by the primary process is the not uncommon dream which only requires symbolic interpretation of its manifest content for its underlying wish to be obvious.

9. Insofar as an object is being used as a symbol by the primary process the significance it has depends entirely on the object it represents and not at all on its own intrinsic nature. When as a result of the use of the mechanisms of projection and denial an object in external reality acquires the cathexis of an internal object the fact that it may be totally inappropriate to fulfil the functions of the object it symbolizes is irrelevant.

10. If used by the secondary process the symbol remains related to the outside world and symbol-formation leads to a widening of the individual's libidinal interests. The fact that symbol-formation is a process capable of indefinite repetition (see para. 4 above) leads to the possibility of an ever-increasing extension of the individual's 'outer world', to his being able to find satisfaction in objects and activities increasingly remote from his primary instinctual interests. This is the process referred to by Jones in his description of civilization as a never-ending series of symbolic substitutions.

11. An object can only be used as a symbol by the secondary process if it is capable of giving real satisfaction, and hence there is no tendency to distortion of the symbol and denial of its actual nature. Reading can symbolize oral activity and become a sublimation only because real knowledge and real enjoyment can be obtained from books. I am well aware that there is something question-begging about this use of the word 'real' and that an important problem lies behind the ability of symbolic equivalents to give enjoyment. It can probably only happen when the relationship to the symbol resembles an object-relationship in involving interaction between subject and symbol and being capable of progressive development.

12. Words are a special class of symbols, which, when operat-

ing as words, form part of the secondary process. They arise in exactly the same way as do other symbols, by displacement of cathexis from the imago of the object onto the imago of the word. In the development of the individual the connexion between word and object is established by habitual association (temporal contiguity). The ultimate reason why any particular word symbolizes its referent is usually only explicable historically, though the number of words which owe their currency to 'sound symbolism' and an intrinsic aptness for their meaning is apparently much greater than the small but well-known group of onomatopoeic words (Jespersen, *Language*, Chap. 20). Words owe their special significance to three characteristics which enable them to be differentiated from other symbols:

(*a*) Their immediate symbolic connexions remain conscious; the person using a word knows what he is symbolizing by it— this notwithstanding the fact that he may be, and only too often is, under a misapprehension as to the meaning it has for his audience.

(*b*) The displacement of cathexis is always partial, the word remaining distinguishable from what it signifies.

(*c*) They are conventionalized symbols. The way in which they are acquired, that is in the simplest instance, by the child repeatedly hearing their sound made in connexion with what they signify leads to the development of a community of symbols, i.e. to a tendency for each individual to use symbols which are common to him and to the other members, both past and present, of his group. It is this that makes possible the transmission of knowledge, morality, etc., from one individual and generation to another. It is this, furthermore, that explains the importance of words in conscious thinking. Freud's statement (1923) that the essential difference between an unconscious idea and a pre-conscious idea is that the latter has been 'brought into connexion with verbal images' is another way of saying that pre-conscious and conscious ideas are communicable and that the ego is that part of the mind which is concerned with object-relationships. Incidentally, I take the phrase 'brought into connexion with verbal images' to mean that pre-conscious and conscious ideas can, when the wish or need arises, be verbalized and not that conscious thought is always verbal. There are, after all, non-verbal modes of communication, nor, even inside the analytical situation, are object-relationships ever conducted on a purely verbal basis.

57

13. Although words have such a close connexion with ego-development and the capacity for object-relationships, their genetic relationship to other classes of symbols is shown by the fact that under certain conditions they lose their three differentiating characteristics and are treated exactly like other symbols. The classic examples of this are dreams and schizophrenic thinking, in both of which words are used by the primary process and (a) acquire meanings of which the individual is unaware, (b) carry the complete cathexes of the objects they normally only signify, and (c) become interchangeable substitutes for one another. 'They transfer their cathexes to one another without remainder' (Freud, 1915). Another example is the neologizing tendency of the schizoid philosopher or psychologist, who is unconsciously using words to create a private inner world. It is probable, indeed, that all disturbances in the capacity for object-relationships are reflected in impairment of the capacity to use words intelligibly. The issue is, however, complicated by a number of social and educational factors which influence verbalization and communication.

14. It is the fact that words can symbolize instinctive acts and objects and carry cathexes ultimately derived from them which makes psycho-analytical treatment possible. As Milner (1952) has pointed out, the 'fundamental rule' that the patient should try to put into words all that he is aware of implies 'that words are in fact symbols by means of which the world is comprehended . . . in the daily battle with our patients over the transference we are asking them to accept a symbolic relation to the analyst instead of a literal one, to accept the symbolism of speech and talking about their wants rather than taking action to satisfy them directly.' Sharpe (1940) in her 'Examination of Metaphor' has described vividly how the metaphors used by patients can be analysed in the same way as the symbols occurring in their dreams and how the emotions which accompanied bodily processes in infancy can be reproduced in speech.

SUMMARY

Symbolism is not inherited, nor is it exclusively 'the language of the unconscious'. Symbols arise by displacement of cathexis from the imagos of objects of primary instinctual interest onto the imagos of objects that have been perceived in the outside world. Once formed, a symbol may be used by either the primary or the secondary process. Insofar as it is used by the primary process its meaning becomes independent of the object it originally represented and it becomes implicated in the fantasy-systems which underlie neurosis and dreaming. Insofar, on the other hand, as it is used by the secondary process, the symbol continues to represent the appropriate object in the outside world and it becomes part of the conscious and unconscious imaginative processes that subserve the development of a sense of reality. I have followed Klein and Isaacs in assuming that the sense of reality is subserved or supported by fantasy, but have suggested that the word 'imagination' might be used to distinguish reality-enhancing fantasies from those which maintain illusory, neurotic substitutes for reality. I have included words among the symbols which subserve the secondary process and have attempted to define the ways in which they can be differentiated from other symbols. I have, in particular, stressed their close connexion with consciousness and with the capacity for object-relationships, a connexion which depends on the fact that verbalization is an important, though not the only, mode of communication between objects.

I have followed Milner and Kubie in taking this wider view of the nature of symbolism and have raised the following objections to restriction of the concept to the defensive use of symbols by the primary process:

1. That it implies that the modes of conscious and unconscious mental activity are qualitatively absolutely different and ignores the implications of Freud's statement that 'the ego is that part of the id which has been modified by the direct influence of the external world'. As Kubie (1953) has said, 'There are no such discontinuities in nature as those who put the symbolism of dreams in a category of its own would seem to imply'.

2. That Jones in his classic paper on symbolism really made a distinction between two different kinds of affect with which symbols might be invested and not one between two different kinds of symbolism.

3. That it implies an antithesis between fantasy and reality which ignores the fact that imagination is necessary for a full appreciation of reality.

4. That the concept of sublimation presupposes that symbol-formation is an important aspect of ego-development.

5. That analytical technique presupposes that the analyst, the

analytical situation, and the words used in analysis are all symbols.

6. That the idea that symbolism is inherited implies either the inheritance of acquired ideas or the existence of a collective unconscious.

5

The Nature and Function of the Analyst's Communication to the Patient[1]

Susanne Langer in her study of symbolism, *Philosophy in a New Key*, observes that 'the great contribution of Freud to the philosophy of mind has been the realization that human behaviour is not only a food-getting strategy, but is also a language; that every move is at the same time a gesture'. By this I understand her to mean two things. First, that psychoanalysis has shown that human behaviour is actuated not only by the need to satisfy instinctual impulses by using appropriate objects but also by a need to maintain a meaningful contact with these objects; and secondly, that human activity is intrinsically symbolic, and comprises an attempt to communicate something. An essential part of her thesis is that the various 'impractical', apparently unbiological activities of man, such as religion, magic, art, dreaming, and symptom-formation—i.e. just those aspects of human life which have become the peculiar domain of psycho-analytical research—arise from a basic human need to symbolize and communicate, and are really languages.

Although I think that Langer is right in this view of psychoanalysis, and would indeed be inclined to add that Freud initiated a revolution in our capacity to communicate by making us aware of previously unrecognized attempts at communication, it is, I believe, also true that theoretical formulations of psycho-analysis have a tendency not to do full justice to the communicative aspects of human behaviour. The reason for this lies in the nature and history of metapsychology. Metapsychology is based on the assumption of a psychic apparatus which is conceived of as a model analogous to a single, isolated central nervous system. Within this apparatus certain

[1] Contribution to the Symposium 'The Theory of Technique' held at the Centenary Scientific Meetings of the British Psycho-Analytical Society on 5 May 1956. First published in the *Int. J. Psycho-Anal.* (1956), **37.**

structures are assumed to exist, to have certain relations one with another, and to be invested with libido and aggression derived from instinctual sources. Some of these structures, such as the ego and object-representations, are conceived of as being related to objects in the external world and to be the result of the impingement of external reality on a primitive undifferentiated apparatus, but, strictly speaking, metapsychology is concerned with these psychical representations and precipitates of the external world, not with the external world itself or with the interaction between the subject and his external objects. For instance, the term 'object-cathexis' refers to the libidinal investment of an object-imago, not to any transmission of libido to the object itself. For this reason the knowledge and theories that we have about the inter-relationships between individuals, and, in particular, about the relationship between patient and analyst, have never been satisfactorily incorporated into metapsychological theory. Rapaport pointed out in 1953 that a metapsychological theory of technique and therapy does not exist, and suggested that an essential prerequistie of such a theory would be clarification of the metapsychological status of affects. Now although Schilder, Brierley, and others have pointed out that affects play an essential part in communication between individuals and in the interplay between internal and external reality, and although the clinical importance of affects in the analytical situation is clearly recognized, none of the various analytical theories of affects reviewed by Rapaport attaches central importance to what is to my mind the most obvious and important fact about an affect—the fact that it is perceptible by others and has an intrinsic tendency to evoke either an identical or complementary affective response in the perceiving object. It seems to me unlikely that a satisfactory metapsychology of technique will be formulated until this fact is taken into account, that is, until we can formulate ideas about the relationships between individuals with the same precision as we can ideas about relations to objects. Until such time our theoretical formulations are bound to give preference to the structural and economic aspects of psychical life at the expense of the communicative.

It will, I hope, be clear that I am not questioning the validity or legitimacy of classical metapsychology or suggesting that it should be replaced by a metapsychology of interpersonal relations. Not only would to do so be a denial of the value of the psychopathology we use daily in our interpretative work with patients; it would also be methodologically incorrect. Even though man is a social animal whose psychical life is primarily concerned with his relations with his objects, each individual is also a separate psychobiological entity with a continuous and independent existence and awareness of self. As a result a conceptual framework within which to formulate hypotheses about the intrapsychic processes and genetic development of single individuals is a scientific necessity. However, there is, I believe, also a need for a related frame of reference arising from the study of the interrelationships between individuals and the means of communication between them. Such a metapsychology of interpersonal relations would prove particularly valuable in clarifying our theories of symbolism, affects, and technique.

At the risk of appearing to digress from the main theme of this paper, I should like to give an example which will, I hope, help to clarify the point I am trying to make. When a baby cries, the cry can be viewed psychologically in two different ways. We can consider it as an event occurring in a field which includes not only the baby but also its mother, or as an experience in the baby's individual psychology. In the former case, the cry is objectively a communication, since it acts as a sign-stimulus to the mother who has an instinctive tendency to respond to it. In the latter case, the cry is certainly a discharge-phenomenon, but we can only view it as subjectively a communication, if and when we are entitled to assume that the mother is psychically represented in the infant's mind. In other words, from the point of view of a psychology of interpersonal relations the infant's affects have a communicative function from the beginning, while from the point of view of individual psychology they do so only after the infant's objects have become psychically represented in the infant's mind.

In *The Ego and the Id* (1923), Freud himself provided the linking idea between the psychology of the individual and the psychology of interpersonal relations. This is the idea that the development of the ego is intimately related to the establishment of object-relations, that the 'ego is that part of the id which has been modified by the direct influence of the external world'. That this external world primarily comprises objects with which the individual has had communication is suggested by his further statement that the essential difference between

an unconscious idea and a preconscious idea is that the latter
has been 'brought into connexion with verbal images'. Now
since words are all learned *from* objects and their primary
function is to communicate *with* objects, this statement implies
that the essential quality of preconscious, and therefore conscious, ideas is that they are communicable and that the ego is
that part of the id which is concerned with communication with
objects. The importance of communication arises from the fact
that the capacity for interpersonal relations is not simply a
matter of being able to use objects to satisfy libidinal impulses—
a food-getting strategy in Susanne Langer's phrase—but is the
ability to maintain a reciprocal relation between self and
object before, during, and after the consummatory acts appropriate to the particular relationship. It also involves the ability
to maintain a living internal psychical relationship with the
object during its physical absence. In other words it is the
ability to keep in contact and communication with objects that
are realistically conceived and are recognized as separate from
the self.

Now the purpose of psycho-analytical treatment is to establish, restore, or increase the patient's capacity for object
relationships and to correct various distortions thereof. The
analyst's various technical procedures are designed to establish
a (special form of) relationship between himself and the patient.
The first thing he does is to provide a setting within which this
relationship can develop. This comprises, among other things,
a quiet room with a couch and a chair behind it, a closed door,
regular and frequent appointments—and himself. This setting
is itself a communication to the patient, since its details are all
signs that the analyst intends taking up a certain attitude towards the patient, that he intends to listen to him, to concern
himself with him without requiring the patient to be concerned
with him, and to protect the contact between them from external
interruption or distraction. In other words, he tells the patient
that he intends to provide one component part of an object-
relationship, a person who will maintain a steady and sustained
interest in *his* object, the patient. He does this, then, in the
first instance by means of *signs*—I am here using the word
'sign' as a technical, semantic term—which indicate the existence of a particular psychological situation. The position of the
analyst's chair in relation to the patient's couch signifies the
analyst's preparedness to listen to the patient, his arrange-

ments about times of sessions, his preparedness to continue to do so, etc. These details are all primarily signs of the analyst's contribution to the establishment of a relationship between himself and the patient, this notwithstanding the fact that the patient may also use any particular detail as a symbol with which to represent specific ideas within his own mind.

I have here made use of the distinction drawn by logicians between signs and symbols. Signs indicate the existence or presence of some process, object, or condition, while symbols refer to or represent conceptions of processes, objects, or conditions. Psychological signs are also signals, since their function is to communicate to a responding object. A baby's cry is not only a sign that there is a baby in distress; it is also a signal of distress, which tends to evoke an appropriate response in its mother. Signs seem to play a fundamental part in communication of affects, since most forms of emotional expression are innate and are immediately comprehensible without recourse to symbolic interpretation. Dreams and symptoms, on the other hand, are symbols, since they refer to, and are only comprehensible in relation to, conceptions existing in the patient's mind. The words used in analysis are also symbols, since they refer to ideas in the patient's and analyst's mind, but the inflections and tones of speech are signs, since they indicate the speaker's affective state.

After the analyst has introduced the patient into the analytical situation, explicit, symbolic communication begins. The analyst invites the patient to talk to him, listens and, from time to time, he himself talks. When he talks, he talks not to himself nor about himself *qua* himself but to the patient about the patient. His purpose in talking is to extend the patient's awareness of himself by pointing out that certain ideas and feelings, which the patient has not communicated, are part of, and relevant to, his present psychological state. The patient has previously been unaware of these ideas, or, if he has been aware of them, he has been unaware of their relevance. In other words, the analyst tries to widen the patient's endopsychic perceptual field by informing him of details and relations within the total configuration of his present mental activity, which for defensive reasons he has been unable to notice or communicate himself.

The analyst is able to do this, largely, though not entirely, because he assumes that although the patient may be consciously only talking to and about himself, he is also unconsciously trying to satisfy his need for an object-relationship by making contact with the analyst. As a result the patient's communications tend to be concerned with the analyst, in the same way as the analyst's are concerned with the patient. The difference between the two is that the patient's conception of the analyst is profoundly influenced by projection on to him of various internal imagos, dating from his past, to which he is attached at the expense of external objects, whereas the analyst's conception of the patient is relatively undisturbed by projections. As a result the analyst's communications to the patient tend to be concerned precisely with his feelings and ideas about the analyst, and with the discrepancy between them and the actual reality of the relationship between patient and analyst. These transferred, discrepant feelings, which consist of unadmitted, inadmissible wishes and phantastic fears, are what prevent the patient from making realistic contact with the analyst and establishing an anxiety-free relationship with him. They are, of course, the same wishes and fears which disturb his capacity for interpersonal relations in everyday life. The analyst's successive interpretations help the patient increasingly to discriminate between his phantastic and infantile preconceptions of the analyst and the reality of his present relationship with him, and, therefore, make it progressively easier for him to become aware of his thoughts and to communicate them to the analyst. His drive to do this is his wish, which has previously been frustrated in so far as he has been ill and therefore isolated, to have a relationship within which he can share experience. The analytical situation enables the patient to communicate, share, and bring into relation with an object, feelings, memories, and thoughts which have previously been repressed or which, even if they have been in a sense conscious, have been experienced in neurotic isolation. Since these communications are predominantly verbal, the analytical process brings previously unconscious and unformulated ideas 'into connexion with verbal images'. The fact that the analyst is more tolerant and realistic than the internal imagos which comprise the patient's superego permits ideas, which had previously been repressed, to be verbalized and communicated. One aspect of the communicative function of words is the permissive; comprehension of an idea by an object allows the subject to entertain it. In addition the analyst's understanding of the language of dreams, symptoms, phantasies and defences enables him to translate into words unconscious attempts at communication which had previously been incomprehensible, while his knowledge of infantile sexuality and relations enables him to interpret and put at the patient's disposal derivatives of pregenital drives which would never be tolerable or comprehensible in their original unsublimated form.

The patient's increasing capacity to be aware of, communicate, and share his mental life cannot however be attributed solely to the intellectual content of the analyst's verbal communications to him. It is also the result of the fact that every 'correct' interpretation, even when it is, as it should be, entirely free of suggestion or reassurance, contains within it a whole number of additional implicit communications. In addition to an explicit statement about, say, the patient's phantasies or defences, it contains a statement about the analyst himself and his attitude towards the patient. It says, in effect, 'I am still here. I have been listening to you. I understand what you are talking about. I remember what you said yesterday, last week, last month, last year. I have been sufficiently interested to listen, and remember, and understand.' Also 'You are not the only person to have felt this way. You are not incomprehensible. I am not shocked. I am not admonishing you or trying to get you to confrom to any ideas of my own as to how you should feel or behave.' The first group comprises a statement of the analyst's interest in the patient as another human being and of his ability to understand him. The second gives the patient permission to be himself and tells him that it is possible to have a relationship with another person without violation of his personality and intrinsic capacity for growth.

Now this implicit statement is a sign of the analyst's interest in and concern for the patient, of his capacity to maintain an object-relationship, at least within the confines of the consulting-room. It tells the patient the one thing that he needs to know about the analyst, and it is the analyst's major contribution to making the relationship between himself and the patient a real and not an illusory relationship. It is an affective communication and, as is characteristic of affective communications, it is made by signs and not by symbols. Although explicit, symbolic communication would be possible, it would also be useless, since it would be an attempt to convey something that the patient can only credit in so far as he has already acquired a capacity for object-relationships. Indeed, many patients would assume that the only possible motive the analyst could have for verbalizing his interest in the patient would be that it was insincere.

In addition therefore to their symbolic function of communicating ideas, interpretations also have the sign-function of conveying to the patient the analyst's emotional attitude towards him. They combine with the material setting provided by the analyst to form the analyst's affective contribution to the formation of a trial relationship, within which the patient can recapture the ability to make contact and communication with external objects. This trial relationship is accompanied by introjection of an unidealized 'good' object and widening and strengthening of the patient's ego.

6

An Enquiry into the Function of Words in the Psycho-analytical Situation[1]

In this paper I shall attempt to formulate certain ideas about the function of words in the psycho-analytical situation. In doing so I shall continue a line of thought that I began in my paper on symbolism (Chapter 4 in the present collection), in which, following Milner (1952) and Kubie (1953), I took the view that it is misleading to restrict the analytical concept of symbolism to the use of symbols by the primary process, and suggested that words should be included within the general category of symbols even though they can be differentiated from other symbols on the grounds: (*a*) that their immediate symbolic connexions remain conscious, (*b*) that the displacement of cathexis from the thing-representation is only partial, the word remaining linked to and yet distinguishable from its referent, and (*c*) that they are conventionalized. These differentiating characteristics enable words to be used by the secondary process for purposes of communication even though they also continue to carry cathexes derived from instinctual sources. In the last paragraph of my paper on symbolism I suggested that it is this dual function of words that makes psycho-analytical treatment possible.

Before coming to the main argument of this present paper I must mention that my contribution to the Freud Centenary Symposium on the Theory of Technique (here printed as Chapter 5) was based on an earlier draft of this paper and that several paragraphs and sentences are common to both. However, my contribution to the Symposium was designed for a specific purpose and occasion and was limited to a period of twenty minutes. As a result it was a highly condensed and in some ways an unsatisfactory statement of various ideas which I

[1] Read before the British Psycho-Analytical Society, 16 January 1957, and published first in the *Int. J. Psycho-Anal.* (1958), **39.**

wish to elaborate in greater detail here. I have called this paper an Enquiry to draw attention to the tentative, almost groping nature of much of the thought that lies behind it.

This paper, like its predecessors, is written from a standpoint which conceives of man as a social animal who, in addition to his drive to self-preservation and self-awareness, is also continuously concerned to maintain himself in a reciprocal, adaptive interrelationship with his objects and which sees psychodynamics as the study of the development of the capacity for interpersonal relations and psychopathology as the study of the ways in which this capacity may break down. I shall start my argument with two very familiar quotations from Freud's *The Ego and the Id* (1923). The first is Freud's definition of the ego as 'that part of the id which has been modified by the direct influence of the external world'. The second is his suggestion that the essential difference between an unconscious idea and a preconscious one is that the latter has been 'brought into connexion with verbal images'. Now since words are all learned *from* objects in the external world and their primary function is to communicate *with* objects, these statements imply (*a*) that the essential quality of preconscious, and therefore conscious, ideas is that they have acquired the quality of communicability and (*b*) that the ego is that part of the id which is concerned with communication with external objects. The importance of communication and, therefore, of speech, as one though not the only mode of communication, arises from the fact that the capacity for interpersonal relations is not simply a matter of being able to use objects to satisfy libidinal wishes but is the ability to maintain a reciprocal relation between self and object before, during, and after the consummatory acts appropriate to the particular relationship. It also involves the ability to maintain a living internal psychical relationship with the object during its physical absence. In other words it is the capacity to keep in contact or communication with objects that are realistically perceived and are recognized as being separate from the self.

Although words are not, of course, the only tools of interpersonal communication—there are indeed numerous occasions on which the use or abuse of words betrays a breakdown in communication on a more simple, emotional level – it is self-evident that they play an important part in all interpersonal relations. Their use implies at least some recognition of the object as separate from the self and, unlike certain other tools of communication such as gestures and emotional expressions (some of which, at least, are innate) they are very obviously learned within the framework of object-relationships. The capacity for speech is certainly a mental function which shows that the id 'has been modified by the direct influence of the external world'. Furthermore, the important part played by words in all psychotherapeutic procedures shows that they can be a major vehicle in relationships which can alter the participants profoundly. Psycho-analytical therapy in particular shows that they can be used for the expression and resolution of infantile conflicts, including those dating from before the patient's acquisition of speech. The way in which this last can happen has been beautifully described by Ella Sharpe in her paper on Metaphor (1940).

One special function of words is their permissive function, which bears a relation to their communicative function analogous to that of the superego to the ego. The acquisition of speech within the framework of object relations leads, as a result of the introjection of objects, to the formation of inner sanctions permitting the formulation and expression of certain ideas and inner prohibitions preventing the formulation and expression of other ideas, which become repressed. Formulation and communication of a previously unconscious idea involves, therfore, the overcoming of an internal resistance deriving from the superego—or, to state the same thing in terms of fantasy, defiance of an internal object. This is why the expression by the analysand of a previously unadmitted idea is preceded by anxiety, or an increase of defences against anxiety, which is followed by a sense of release when the idea is finally communicated. This is also why the formulation of original ideas, even those of a scientific and impersonal nature, requires moral courage. The analysand the the original thinker or artist both have to face the fear of being neither understood nor approved. They face the fear of isolation from objects, both internal and external. To put the matter the other way round, comprehension and toleration of an idea by the analyst gives the analysand permission to entertain it. I speak here of the analysand acquiring permission to *entertain* previously repressed ideas rather than to *hold* them, since it can obviously happen that the patient has to entertain an idea consciously before he can discover that it is not true, or entertain a wish to do something before he can discover that he does not really want to do it.

In this paper, however, I do not intend to consider the part played by words in the analysand's internal economy, and shall not discuss in any detail the rôle they play in intra-psychic communication, integration, and the growth of self-awareness. Instead, I shall restrict myself to certain aspects of the inter-communication between analyst and analysand, with special reference to the verbal communications made by the former to the latter.

The purpose of psycho-analytical treatment is to increase the patient's capacity for object-relationships, and the analyst's various technical procedures are designed to establish a special form of relationship between himself and the patient, in which the analyst, while remaining an external object, can also become the temporary representative and personification of the various internal figures dating from his past to whom he is attached at the expense of his capacity for conscious relationships with present-day external objects.

The analyst's first contribution to the formation of a relationship between himself and the patient is the provision of a setting within which this relationship can develop. This setting includes, among other things, a quiet room with a couch in it, a closed door, regular and frequent appointments—and the analyst himself. This setting is itself a communication to the patient, since its details are all signs that the analyst is preparing to take up a certain attitude towards him, that he intends to listen to him, to concern himself with him without requiring him to be concerned with the analyst, and to protect the contact between them from external distraction. This communication is non-verbal and is a silent indication that he intends to provide one component part of an object-relationship, a person who will maintain a steady and sustained interest in *his* object, the patient. He does this, then, in the first instance by means of signs—I am here using the word 'sign' as a technical, semantic term—which indicates the existence of a particular psychological situation. The position of the analyst's chair in relation to the patient's couch signifies the analyst's preparedness to listen to the patient, his arrangements about times of sessions, his willingness to continue to do so, etc. These details are all signs of the analyst's contribution to the establishment of a relationship between himself and the patient, this notwithstanding the fact that the patient may also use any particular detail as a symbol with which to represent specific unconscious ideas within his own mind.

I have here made use of the distinction drawn by logicians between signs and symbols. Signs indicate the existence or presence of some process, object, or condition, while symbols refer to or represent conceptions of processes, objects, or conditions. Psychological signs are also signals, since their function is to communicate to a responding object. A baby's cry is not only a sign that there is a baby in distress: it is also a signal of distress, which tends to evoke an appropriate response in its mother. Similarly signs of sexual interest are signals which tend to evoke either a response or alternatively defences against making a response. Signs play an especially important part in communication of affects, since many forms of emotional expression are probably innate and are immediately comprehensible without recourse to symbolic interpretation. Dreams and symptoms on the other hand are symbolic modes of expression, since they refer to, and are only comprehensible in relation to, conceptions existing in the patient's mind. The words used in analysis are also symbols, since they refer to ideas in the analyst's and patient's mind, but the inflections and tones of speech are signs since they indicate directly the speaker's affective state.

In describing the provision of a setting as the analyst's first therapeutic activity I am, of course, following Winnicott (1958) and Balint (1952), who in different ways and from somewhat differing standpoints have both stressed the importance of the setting and atmosphere within which the analytical process takes place. This setting provides the framework within which explicit, symbolic communication develops. The analyst invites the patient to talk to him, listens, and from time to time talks himself. When he talks, he talks neither to himself nor about himself *qua* himself, but to the patient about the patient. His purpose in doing so is to enlarge the patient's self-awareness by drawing his attention to certain ideas and feelings, which the patient has not explicitly communicated, but which are nonetheless part of and relevant to his present psychological state. These ideas, which the analyst is able to observe and formulate because they are implicit in what the patient has said or in the way in which he has said it, have either been unconscious, or, if

73

they have been conscious, it has been without any awareness of their present and immediate relevance. In other words the analyst seeks to widen the patient's endopsychic perceptual field by informing him of details and relations within the total configuration of his present mental activity which for defensive reasons he is unable to perceive or communicate himself.

The analyst is able to do this, largely though not entirely, because he assumes that although the patient may consciously only be talking to and about himself he is unconsciously also trying to satisfy his need for an object-relationship by making contact with the analyst. As a result his communications tend to be concerned, consciously or unconsciously, with the analyst, just as those of the analyst tend to be concerned with the patient. The difference between the two is that the patient's conception of the analyst is profoundly influenced by projection on to him of the various internal imagos, dating from his past, to which he is attached at the expense of external objects, whereas the analyst's conception of the patient is relatively undisturbed by projection. The analyst's communications to the patient tend, therefore, to be concerned precisely with his feelings and ideas about the analyst and the way in which they reflect his experiences and fantasies of infantile and childhood objects. They progressively help the patient to discriminate between his fantastic and infantile preconceptions of the analyst and other figures in his present life and the reality of his adult relationship with them, and therefore make it progressively easier for him to become aware of his thoughts and communicate them to the analyst. His drive to do this is his wish, which has previously been frustrated in so far as he has been ill and therefore isolated, to have a relationship within which he can share experience. The analytical situation enables the patient to communicate, share, and bring into relation with an object, feelings, memories, and thoughts which have previously been either repressed and unconscious or split off and only experienced in states of dissociation. Since these communications are predominantly verbal, the analytical process brings previously unconscious and unformulated ideas 'into connexion with verbal images'. The fact that the analyst is more tolerant and realistic than the infantile imagos which comprise his superego permits ideas, which have previously been repressed, to be verbalized and communicated. In addition the analyst's under-

74

standing of the language of dreams, symptoms, fantasies, and defences enables him to translate into words unconscious attempts to communicate which had previously been inaccessible and incomprehensible, while his knowledge of infantile sexuality and the nature of infantile object relations enables him to facilitate the symbolization of pregenital drives which had been intolerable to the patient's ego in their original unsublimated form.

The patient's increasing capacity to be aware of, communicate, and share his mental life cannot, however, be attributed solely to the intellectual content of the analyst's verbal communications. It is also the result of the fact that every correct interpretation, even when it is, as it should be, entirely free of reassurance or suggestion, contains within it a whole number of additional implicit communications about the analyst and his attitude towards the patient. In addition to enlightening the patient about, say, his fantasies or defences, it also indicates that the analyst is still present and awake, that he has been listening and has understood what the patient has been talking about, that he remembers what the patient has said during the present and previous sessions—amd that he has been sufficiently interested to listen and remember and understand. Furthermore, the fact that it is an interpretation and not a reassurance or admonition indicates that his feelings are neither unique nor incomprehensible and that the analyst is neither shocked nor trying to get him to conform to any preconceptions of his own as to how he should feel or behave. In other words it tells the patient (a) that the analyst is interested in him as another human being and is capable of understanding him, and, (b) that it is possible to have a relationship with another person without violation or distortion of his own subjective experience and intrinsic capacity for growth. I should perhaps stress that I am here referring to interpretations which are correct not only in respect of content but also in respect of timing and affect.

These implicit statements are signs of the analyst's interest in the patient, of his capacity to maintain an object-relationship, at least within the confines of his consulting room. They tell the patient the one thing that he needs to know about the analyst and are the analyst's major contribution to making the contact between himself and the patient a real and not an illusory relationship. They constitute an affective communication, and, as is characteristic of affective communications, it is made by signs and not by symbols. Although it could be communicated explicitly in words, it would be both irrelevant and useless to do so, since it would be an attempt to convey something that the patient can only credit in so far as he has already acquired the capacity for object-relationships. In the transference neuroses, belief in external objects is sufficiently developed to prevent the patient ever seriously doubting the analyst's concern and interest, while in the narcissistic neuroses distrust of external objects constitutes a major therapeutic problem. In the former, therefore, explicit statement of the analyst's interest is useless because it is unnecessary: in the latter it is useless because it would not be believed. Indeed, many such patients would feel that any expression of positive feeling by the analyst was forced and contrived, even if they believed it. The various psychotherapies which use explicit statements of positive feeling by the therapist probably only work by exploiting the patient's capacity to overcome distrust by idealization. In the long run it can only be overcome by signs of real and sustained interest and understanding and not by verbal expression of positive feeling.

In addition, therefore, to their symbolic function of communicating ideas which increase the patient's insight and self-awareness, interpretations also have the sign-function of conveying to the patient the analyst's affective attitude towards him. They combine with the material setting provided by the analyst to form the analyst's affective contribution to the establishment of a trial relationship in which distrust can be overcome and the patient can increase his ability to make contact and communication with external objects.

In the previous section I have touched on three problems, which if pursued at any length would lead us far from the restricted theme of this present paper. These are (a) the distinction between signs and symbols, and the part played by sign-communication in human relationships in general and the analytical situation in particular, (b) the part played by the analyst's emotional attitude in overcoming the patient's distrust of objects, and (c) the nature and psychological status of the analyst's therapeutic attitude. Before returning to the subject of words in the psycho-analytical situation I should, however, like to comment briefly on these three topics.

The clear-cut distinction I have drawn between signs and symbols would not, I believe, prove tenable in the precise form I have made it, if more detailed semantic and clinical analysis of the two concepts were attempted. The reason for this is that the concept 'sign' embraces two notions which are not necessarily inseparable. These are (*a*) the idea that a sign indicates the actual presence of something, in contrast to a symbol, which only refers to or represents it, and (*b*) the idea that a sign can be understood directly without symbolic interpretation. On every occasion that I have used the term 'sign', I have done so to refer to something which indicates the presence of what it signifies, but the various 'signs' I have mentioned differ in respect of the way in which they are perceived and apprehended. A baby's cry is, most probably, understood and responded to directly and instinctively, and so, probably, are the tones and inflections of speech, but the signs of the analytical setting certainly require some development of the capacity for symbolic thinking before they can be understood. Further analysis of this problem would involve us both in further verbal definitions and distinctions and in clinical examination of *how* affects are expressed, communicated, and perceived. For the purposes of this present paper we need only recognize that they are.

The idea that the analyst's affective attitude helps to dispel the tendency to distrust in narcissistic patients is based on the assumption that distrust cannot be understood in terms of projection of hostility alone, but that it is also a manifestation of the hypersensitivity of the narcissistic ego. Objects and circumstances that are felt to threaten the integrity of the ego always tend to evoke hatred and suspicion, and this defensive reaction is easily aroused in patients who fear that positive contact with an object involves submission to the object's conception of psychical reality and violation or distortion of the subject's own experience of self. In so far as this fear is present the psychoanalytical situation itself may seem peculiarly dangerous, since the analyst's interpretations may be felt as an attempt to impose a certain view of psychical reality and his possession of a psychological theory as evidence that he has a *Weltanschauung* to which he wishes to convert his patients. Furthermore, the very fact that language is derived from external objects and contains within it precipitates of past psychological experience and theories may lead to hatred and suspicion of words themselves. The only patient I have had who openly hated words did so

on the ground that their very existence showed the impossibility of any real understanding between human beings. Only
when she wrote poetry did she feel that words were her own.

Various attempts have been made to define the nature of the
analyst's therapeutic attitude, but they usually fail, I believe,
in implying a greater degree of either detachment or involvement than is usually either present or desirable. They range
from the idea that the analyst remains a completely detached
observer who operates in a state of pure intellect entirely undisturbed by feeling to the opposite idea that it is in the last
resort the analyst's love that cures the patient. On the other
hand some of the most apt descriptions of the analyst's attitude
fail to define it psychologically at all. For instance the phrase
'benevolent neutrality', which grammatically is an oxymoron,
a combination of two contradictory terms, implies both that it is
an affective attitude and that it is not. My assumption in this
paper is that it is a sentiment, in McDougall's (1931) and
Shand's sense of the term, that is, an organized, enduring dis-
position of emotional tendencies, which is maintained more or
less consistently, even though it may suffer passing disturbances
due to fatigue, preoccupation, etc. This sentiment can be
thought of as a specific development of that component part of
the capacity for interpersonal relations which makes interest,
concern and empathy for the object a natural and spontaneous
activity.

The analyst's ability to maintain this sentiment is the result of
a number of factors, including (a) the various drives and identifications which have led him to choose psycho-analysis as a
profession and enable him to get satisfaction from it; (b) the
analytical setting, which is adapted to his needs as well as to
the patient's. For instance, it protects him from external distraction just as much as it does the patient. It also restricts to
known and tolerable limits the contact he has with the patient.
(c) The fact that the has several patients, thereby diminishing
the intensity of his involvement with any one of them, and (d)
his ability to operate a split in his ego, analogous to that required of the patient (Sterba, 1934), which makes his relationship to his patients an *imaginative* participation in their inner and
outer life rather than a direct involvement with them. I have
selected these four factors for mention since, taken together,
they draw attention to the part played in the psycho-analytical
situation by the analyst's capacities and needs.

Although the interest and understanding felt by the analyst is, either consciously or unconsciously, perceived by the patient, it is just as likely to be distorted or denied by him as is any other aspect of the analytical setting. Perception by the patient that he is being understood may, for instance, be used as the basis for a fantasy of complete union with the analyst, as a patient of mine did when she reacted to interpretations which struck her as particularly understanding by going into blissful, hypomanic states of what she called 'transcendental harmony'. In contrast, she treated interpretations which she was not prepared to accept as deliberate sadistic attacks. Less dramatically, other patients may overvalue the feeling of being psychologically understood as a defence against recognizing bodily needs and feelings of physical deprivation. On the other hand, patients who equate being understood with being devoured or penetrated may deny that they are being understood or attempt to make it impossible for the analyst to understand them. Alternatively they may try to prove that the understanding is either insincere and hypocritical or is motivated only by intellectual or financial considerations. They may also try to make the analyst feel that he is failing to understand them in the hope of undermining his self-esteem by making him feel that he lacks a quality of mind essential to being a good analyst. In this they are behaving like revengeful children who try to make their parents feel that they lack parental feelings. Such patients incidentally provide another reason against the analyst expressing his interest in the patient.

To return to the main theme of this paper, I should like to discuss briefly three other factors which influence the total meaning attached by the patient to the analyst's interpretations.

The first is that the patient will, at times, use speech as a symbolic substitute for infantile sexual activities. At such times he will not only use his own speech to discharge oral, anal, or phallic drives, or to gain exhibitionist or narcissistic pleasure, but will also endow the analyst's speech with identical or complementary meanings. In other words he will react to the analyst's speech as though it too had these pregenital meanings or alternatively will endow listening to it with oral, masochistic, or voyeuristic significance.

The second arises from the fact that, logically speaking,

79

every statement implies two other classes of statements, the assumptions that have to be made before the original statement can be formulated and the corollary statements that can be deduced from it. It follows from this that every interpretation the analyst makes implies a whole number of assumptions about mental functioning in general and the patient's individual psychology in particular and also a number of deductions that can be made from it. Patients seem to vary considerably in their capacity to apprehend the full implications of single interpretations. This variation is not only a function of intelligence but also depends on the various factors which influence the rate at which 'working through' takes place. The fact that every interpretation logically implies a number of other interpretations is important in considering the process of interpretation during the course of an analysis, since each interpretation can then be seen as a member of an interpretative series, which tends to assume those that have preceded it and to foreshadow those that will follow it. In other words each interpretation can be though of as a detail of a total interpretative pattern which emerges during the course of the analysis. I am not, of course, suggesting that this total pattern will necessarily ever become explicit either in the form of a 'complete' interpretation by the analyst or of a total insight of the patient's. To suppose so would be to forget that clinical facts are never as orderly as the theories we abstract from them.

The third factor influencing the meaning attached to interpretations is that all words tend to evoke associated images additional to those necessary to comprehend intellectually the idea which the word is being used to convey. These associated images are responsible for the poetry of words and for the fact that all words, even the most abstract, have shades and overtones of meaning and tend to evoke concrete images. Even language which is designed to avoid imaginative reverberations fails to do so since it evokes a feeling of dryness. The fact that the analyst and patient have a language in common means, of course, that they tend to share the same associations to words, but disparity of imaginative associations and resonances can, on occasion, be a source of misunderstanding or distraction. It can, for instance, obviously happen that the analyst unwittingly uses some word or phrase which the patient associates with a particular affective situation quite other than the one to which the analyst was referring. Alternatively a patient may fail to appreciate the full psychological meaning of a word used by the analyst and take it in a more restricted, literal sense than the analyst intends. Thus, a patient failed to realize that the word 'castrated', which his analyst often used, had any connexion with feelings of being emasculated or unmanned psychologically. He assumed that his analyst meant anatomical castration and nothing else. As a result many interpretations he received, though accepted intellectually, lacked psychological reality. In such a case apparent verbal understanding masks a failure in communication. On the other hand, when the analyst succeeds in formulating interpretations in a way that takes cognisance of the patient's imaginative processes and are meaningful at different levels of experience, this does much to establish and maintain contact with the patient as a whole person.

The tendency of words to evoke concrete imagery creates quite peculiar difficulties in patients who have lost the ability to distinguish between words and what they signify, since they tend to react to interpretations as though they were the process that the interpretation refers to and are liable to confuse literal and metaphorical meanings. The only neologistic patient I have ever had developed her highly abstract and tortuous mode of speech to prevent herself being overwhelmed by the concrete imagery and physical sensations which normal, everyday metaphorical speech evoked in her. It is, of course, in schizophrenic and schizoid patients that problems of communication become most apparent, since their tendency to withdrawal, introversion, and distrust is due to ambivalence about the wish to communicate and preoccupation with the hazards that are felt to attach to doing so.

Throughout this paper I have concentrated on the verbal communications made by the analyst and have said little about the verbal behaviour of the patient. As a result I have not discussed the way in which information about the patient's infantile anxiety situations and psychopathology can be deduced from his linguistic habits—a possibility which was first envisaged by Ella Sharpe in her paper 'Psycho-physical Problems revealed in Language: an Examination of Metaphor' (1940), and which has since been confirmed statistically in a series of papers by Lorenz and Cobb (1953). Lorenz (1953) suggests that many of our so-called intuitive judgements of others are in fact based on our unconscious perception and evaluation of their linguistic and syntactical habits, and cites examples of the way in which disturbances in object-relations, self-awareness, affectivity, etc. are reflected in habits of speech. If this is true it follows, on the principle that what is sauce for the goose must also be sauce for the gander, that the patient must also have material available on which to make intuitive evaluations of his analyst.

My reason for giving greater consideration to what the analyst says to the patient than to what the patient says to the analyst has been my conviction that we are more likely to increase our understanding of the dynamics of the analytical process by viewing it as a relationship, albeit of a unique kind, between two persons, than as a situation in which one person observes another. It must be admitted, however, that this view of the analytical process presents certain difficulties, which can easily be avoided if we limit ourselves to the fiction that we simply observe our patients. These difficulties are both of a practical and theoretical nature.

The practical ones arise from the fact that recognition of the analytical situation as a relation between two persons compels us to take the analyst's psychology into account. I have, for instance, mentioned that the analyst's capacity to get satisfaction from his work contributes to his ability to maintain an appropriate emotional attitude to his patients, and that certain details of the analytical setting conform to his needs as much as they do to the patient's. Further analysis of what I have called the analyst's sentiment would, however, require more detailed information about the analyst's subjective experience and the origin of his need to be an analyst than is at present available.

The theoretical difficulties arise from the fact that the problem of communication in the analytical situation is largely a problem of affects, and, as Rapaport (1953) has pointed out, the clinical and theoretical problems involved are of a complexity which 'makes a definitive formulation of an up-to-date theory of affects certainly ill-advised, if not impossible'. Furthermore, Rapaport's review of past and present theories of affects shows that more interest has been shown in affects as tension and discharge phenomena and as endopsychic signals used by the ego in its work of mastering impulses than in their communicative function. In particular, there is only passing reference, via the connexion between affects and empathy, to the assumption made throughout this paper that affects are not only observable but also tend to evoke a response in their observer, and that it is the interaction of affects which is responsible for the sense of contact which is so essential in the analytical situation. I am not, however, claiming that there is anything new in this idea. It is implicit in the clinical concept of 'rapport' and in much of the literature on countertransference. In this paper I have been concerned with the part played by words in maintaining not only intellectual but also affective contact in the analytical situation.

7

On the Defensive Function of Schizophrenic Thinking and Delusion-Formation[1]

The material to be presented in this paper is derived from an analysis which ended with the committal of the patient to a mental hospital, where he was diagnosed schizophrenic. As many analysts would never have started with such a patient, while others would have adopted some modification of technique, probably including management and control of the patient's environment, I must begin by mentioning a number of facts which will, I hope, make it comprehensible that such a patient should have been in analysis and prevent my listeners being distracted from my main theme, which is theoretical, by queries about technique and doubts whether I knew what kind of patient I had on my hands. The relevant facts are, briefly:

(i) The analysis was undertaken on the initiative of the patient's father, who was well aware both that his son had a psychotic illness and that psycho-analysis is a form of treatment designed for neurotic disorders. He knew therefore that his son's treatment was experimental and that he could be given no assurance of a cure.

(ii) Prior to coming to me the patient had not only had E.C.T. and Insulin therapy, but had also been in psychotherapy with a therapist who had actively encouraged him to lead a less secluded life; this had been without much effect.

(iii) Although the material which I shall present stresses the patient's extreme isolation and shows him to have been incapable of functioning for any length of time as an autonomous adult, he remained throughout capable of some independent activity. He could, for instance, travel alone to and from his home country, either by sea or air, and deal adequately with the Police and the Home Office. Furthermore, although he lived alone in London, away from his family, he

[1] Paper read to a meeting of the British Psycho-Analytical Society on 1 June 1960, and to the London Imago Group on 31 January 1961. First published in the *Int. J. Psycho-Anal.* (1962), **43.**

was visited by his parents and siblings on several occasions during the four years in which he was in analysis.

These few facts will, I hope, make it clear that I am, and was from the very beginning, aware of the practical problems involved in treating such a patient. These problems, however, are *not* the subject of my present communication, which is concerned with two closely related theoretical problems: (i) the defensive function of schizophrenic thinking and delusion-formation, and (ii) the schizophrenic's search for an identity and sense of significance.

I wish to discuss certain observations made during the analysis of a young man whose illness resembles in certain striking respects that suffered by Schreber (Freud, 1911). The history of his illness differs, however, from that of Schreber's in three respects that must be defined before I present my material. First, my patient's illness began in adolescence and not in middle age; as a result his father not only played a rôle in the internal drama of his illness but was also a participator in his external life and was actively implicated in every therapeutic measure taken on his behalf. Secondly, whereas in Schreber's case only eighteen months or so elapsed between the time that he fell acutely ill and the emergence of his belief that he was the Redeemer and God's Spouse, the corresponding period in my patient's illness extended over thirteen years. Thirdly, my patient was in psycho-analytical treatment for the last four of the thirteen years which preceded definitive delusion-formation. Freud, it will be remembered, described Schreber's delusional system as an attempt at recovery, as a process of reconstruction by which external reality, from which cathexis had been withdrawn during the initial, acute phase of his illness, became reinvested with significance so that it again became a place in which he could live. In my patient's case this reinvesting of the external world with significance, albeit delusional significance, occurred while he was in analysis, and was indeed in all probability the result of analysis. My material therefore can be divided into two parts, one describing the last three of the thirteen years in which my patient lived in that psychical limbo which Schreber characterized by saying that all the people he met and, I think, all the thoughts he had were 'miracled-up' and 'cursorily improvised'—that is, unreal, insignificant, and irrelevant—and another describing the emergence of a definite delusional system which again gave meaning to my patient's world and his place in it. I shall in addition describe how my patient discovered that his delusional ideas were incompatible with the view of reality held by his fellow men and how he accommodated himself to that discovery.

Mr Y is a tall, heavily built young man, who was 26 when he began psycho-analytical treatment in 1955. I was at that time struck by his awkward and ungainly posture and by the way in which he appeared to have abandoned every device by which human beings endeavour to make ,themselves interesting and acceptable to others. Not only was he without charm, he also took no trouble with his clothes, and gave the impression that he rarely washed. His voice was expressionless and kept to the same monotone regardless of whether he was talking about personal or impersonal matters. That he should either make or see a joke was inconceivable. As he talked it became apparent that he made no distinction between different modes of thought and communication; all his thoughts were of one order, so that he failed to discriminate between those which were factual and those which were fantastic, or between what he perceived and what he conceived, or between ideas which he held and ideas which he entertained. The categories which a normal or neurotic person uses to differentiate between the kinds of thought he is having seemed not to exist for him. This, however, did not mean that everything he thought was equally real and significant or that everything was equally unreal and painfully meaningless. It was just that everything was, as he put it, 'hypothetical', so that nothing mattered more—or less—than anything else. One effect of this loss of discriminating capacity was that no recollection was unequivocally valid. He had the idea that when the ship that brought him to England came into harbour it was met by Bertrand Russell and myself. We had, according to this idea of his, come to ensure that he had a safe journey to London. Yet, although he had this recollection and could, for instance, describe our disguise and the boat in which we had come out to meet his ship, it was to his mind just as likely that this incident had not occurred as that it had. Similarly, he had the idea that he attended a Dr Rycroft for psycho-analytical treatment. It was, however, possible that I was not

Dr Rycroft, or that there were two or more Dr Rycrofts; in any case it didn't really matter whether I was or was not Dr Rycroft, or whether I was singular or plural. The whole matter was 'hypothetical', and no one of the many alternative hypotheses was preferable to any other. His rare visits to the cinema led him to make comments which clearly showed his inability to distinguish what kind of experience he was having. After seeing a humorous film in which Danny Kaye falls in love with his beautiful young female psycho-analyst, his only comment was surprise that such a young and attractive woman should have been allowed to practise.

Mr Y's contention that all his thoughts and perceptions were 'hypothetical' could be regarded quite simply as a consequence of his having withdrawn interest both from external reality—which is how Freud interpreted Schreber's idea that after his world-catastrophe everyone around him was 'cursorily improvised'—and from his own inner psychical reality, but it can, I believe, also be seen to have had an active defensive function. It ensured (*a*) that no aspect of external reality could be considered either as frightening or tempting, and (*b*) that no thought of his could be unequivocally recognized, either by others or himself, as delusional. His sanity, or what was left of it, resided in his doubt, which prevented him from being overwhelmed either by delusional misconceptions of external reality or by his own impulses. It was no accident that in his first interview he told me that, speaking as a philosopher, his considered opinion was that the unconscious is a hypothesis. Rather similarly, if every communication he made or received was devoid of any mode by which it could be categorized as literal or metaphorical, serious or humorous, factual or emotive, no questions of motive, or of nuances and overtones, ever arose, and no one could ever be felt to be loving or hating him, while he himself could never betray love or hate or fear. Bateson *et al.* (1956) have put forward the thesis that a loss of the capacity to distinguish between different modes of communication constitutes the initial disturbance in schizophrenic thinking, and that its function is to enable the patient to deny perceptions of ambivalence both in himself and others.

Although this defence of making everything 'hypothetical' led to Mr Y presenting the classical psychiatric picture of flattening of affect, it was not an absolutely efficient defence. An undercurrent of intense anxiety was perceptible to anyone capable of attuning himself to it. His father was aware of it, and so was I, but neither his mother nor his brother had any inkling of it. Nor had he succeeded in eliminating all signs that he had emotional needs. In the last three years of his analysis the landlady at his lodgings not only registered his unconscious wish to be mothered, but also, for her own reasons, responded to it. As a result his dependence on her to keep him fed, warm, and clothed, and to keep him protected from the demands normally made on grown-up persons, became enormous. This unguarded wish for infantile dependence was revealed to me during the first moments of his treatment. When he lay down on my couch he immediately discovered a position in which he could without discomfort gaze at me, and then gave me one beautiful smile which permanently endeared him to me.

Mr Y could not, of course, remember anything of his early relation to his mother, and consciously he had no kind of feeling for that relationship. Mothers indeed had no place in his scheme of things, and one could have listened indefinitely to his spontaneous associations without ever discovering that such persons exist. In Schreber's case too, mothers were conspicuous by their absence. In analysis, however, Mr Y not only derived considerable gratification from gazing at me, but also felt himself to be refreshed and strengthened by inhaling the various hypnotic and stimulant drugs I exhaled. He did indeed appear to benefit from his contact with me, and it was the improvement in his general condition and appearance, coupled with a marked alleviation of his obsessional rituals, which encouraged his father and myself to continue his treatment. He himself, however, took only a hypothetical interest in the matter.

The absence of any conscious interest in his mother or in any idea of mothers was paralleled by the fact that a thousand-word history of his life and illness written by his father contained only two references to his mother. One described her as 'beautiful, energetic, perhaps too dominant'. The other stated that the patient had been weaned in one day at seven months on account of a sudden illness of hers. The fact that an otherwise meticulous, detailed, and psychologically well-informed document should contain no other references to the patient's mother is one of several pieces of evidence which convince me that my patient grew up in a family which was held together not by normal heterosexual love, but by a façade of conscientious conformity to the ideal of family life, behind which the actual relationships were ambivalent and psychopathologically complex. Unfortunately my information about the various members of the family is insufficient to enable me to formulate clearly what was amiss with this family. My impression is, however, that it would not be possible to attribute Mr Y's illness to his having been brought up by a schizophrenogenic mother; any attempt to formulate a familial aetiology would certainly have to take into account the father's unconscious homosexuality, indications of which will be apparent later in this paper.

Mr Y's recollection of his first five years was that they had been intensely happy. Every moment, he said, had been an adventure, and every familiar object had retained the freshness of a new discovery; the whole world had seemed 'apparelled in celestial light'. This quotation from Wordsworth was his own, not mine. His father too remembers him as a happy child 'not shy, and easily smiling'. And then at 5 the darkness began to set in. He learned to read, and immediately felt like a grown-up. The world of things ceased to be an adventure, and he became intellectually precocious. According to his own account he was reading and understanding Sir James Jeans' *The Mysterious Universe* when he was 8. The literal truth of this may be doubted, but his father reports that he was regularly top of his class at school and was always one or two years ahead of his age. *The Mysterious Universe* certainly too had a profound effect on him; mathematics, philosophy, and astronomy were always his central interests when well, and contributed to his ruminations and delusions when ill. This change from, presumably, a manic-defensive to a schizoid-obsessional organization can be regarded as an infantile precursor of his world-catastrophe in adolescence. It was possibly precipitated by the birth of his sister. That it involved withdrawal of cathexis from objects and their replacement by highly cathected ideas is shown by his conviction that his father at this time underwent a change of person. He came to doubt his father's identity, and believed that he might have doubles. From then on he related himself to imaginary fathers, all of whom were famous mathematicians and philosophers. These included Gauss, Sir James Jeans, Bertrand Russell, and Abel, the Norwegian mathematician who proved that equations of the fifth degree are insoluble. By providing himself with such a galaxy of distinguished ancestors Mr Y again resembled Schreber, who created his ancestors Margraves of Tuscany and Tasmania. My patient preferred a distinguished intellectual descent, partly, but only partly, for social reasons. Unlike Schreber, who lived in a country and at a time which idolized nobility and was obsessed by notions of social status, he came from a country which has no aristocratic tradition and in which sons do not bear their father's surname. This, however, cannot have been the sole reason, since he shifted his allegiances during analysis, and, when sexual and aggressive drives began to re-emerge, took such figures as Khrushchev, Eisenhower, and Joe Louis to himself as fathers.

His family do not appear to have noticed anything amiss when he was 5; they were proud of his intellectual precocity and not until he was 17 did they realize that they had a sick son. One can, I think, be sceptical of the son's story of his sudden trans-formation from an innocent wide-eyed boy into a prematurely serious intellectual. Such a change, if it had occurred at all rapidly, could hardly not have been noticed by his family, and the whole story is in any case obviously tendentious, since it derives its significance from the patient's later conception of himself as someone predestined to save the world. It is, we might say, part of the myth of the childhood of an Intellectual Hero. It can be regarded, however, as a metaphorical descrip-tion of that process, which can be observed in many patients who never become schizophrenic, by which the traumatically lost breast is rediscovered in intellectual ideas and the un-satisfied need to incorporate is assuaged by acquiring know-ledge from men. In such persons, intellectual development, instead of being a manifestation of increased active hetero-sexual mastery of the world, becomes a passive, homosexual defence against oedipal anxiety.

The next step in Mr Y's illness occurred in his eighteenth year, when he had three experiences which I shall describe in what seems to me to be their logical order, though I have no idea whether the chronology is in fact correct. First, he found that his masturbation fantasies had come to centre round the idea of either drowning or strangling a girl in his class at school. Secondly, he collapsed one day weeping and distressed by he knew not what on to his mother's bed in the parental bedroom. Only his father could give him any comfort, but as his father had and could have had no knowledge of what was really troubling him, this comfort went no further than that provided by the conviction that his father wished to help him. Thirdly, he was walking one day along the coast near his home when he saw a fleet of warships out at sea. As he stood watching them he saw them sink without a trace, one by one. This, of course, was his world-catastrophe. What I believe had happened was this. First, he had been appalled at discovering his hatred of women, and became terrified of his size and strength; he must have been nearly full-grown by then, and was certainly already biologically potent. Next he turned to his father for help. His previous development made it impossible for him to do so on a man-to-man basis, and the only pattern of contact available was that of passive homosexual dependence. As a result he had to repress completely his aggressive drives in order to be the helpless and harmless son on whom his father could safely shower parental devotion. This massive repression he experienced as the loss at sea of a fleet of warships. This defence against sadism and aggression involved withdrawal of all significant cathexis from external objects, with the single exception that he retained a passive dependent relationship to his father. As a result he ceased to have any significance or sense of identity apart from that provided by his being his father's son and his father's patient. My impression is that his capacity to retain even this fragment of a relationship was achieved by collusion with his father's unconscious active maternal homosexuality. In this sense Mr Y became his father's spouse just as Schreber became God's. The rays of sunlight with which God aroused voluptuous sensations in his wife Schreber were represented in my patient's illness by the money which his father paid out to provide his son with medical treatments, an expenditure which his father's actual wife understandably resented.

Although Mr Y described his adolescent breakdown in tones of complete indifference, and, for instance, recounted the sinking of the warships as an event which he had—possibly—witnessed, it must in fact have been a period of the greatest distress. During it he became addicted to benzedrine and caffeine, which he took to strengthen himself against the dangers he felt to be threatening him from within and without. He also reversed his sleeping habits, so that he slept while his family was awake and was awake while they slept, thereby restricting his contact with them to a minimum. Attempts to disturb this pattern led to rages. During the period in which he was in analysis he tended to sleep excessively, especially when I was on holiday, and to ignore conventional routines, but he accommodated himself with tolerable success to my time-table.

During the nine years following his acute illness Mr Y had two courses of insulin comas, one course of E.C.T., and a few months of psychotherapy. None of these had any radical effect on him, though he did become free of his addiction to amphetamine and caffeine and had periods in which he was capable of studying for university examinations. Both his treatments and his studies were undertaken on the initiative of his father, who throughout this period took up an active therapeutic and protective attitude towards him. Something of this attitude is perhaps shown by the following quotations from the report on Mr Y which his father wrote for me, and which I have already mentioned. (i) 'Notable symptoms: Seclusion, very little contacts with people outside family. Irregular sleeping times. Various ceremonials, sometimes washing, frequent changing of underwear, etc. Fear indoors of sharp corners with as a result a peculiar cautious way of walking, fears for the safety of family members.' (ii) 'I am telling him that an initial belief in the unconscious, etc., is not indispensable, only a benevolent, if sceptical attitude, and an honest will to co-operate, and that with these he will have good chances of recovery. All the same I suspect that he has a quite inordinate fear of his own primitive impulses, and that it will perhaps not be an easy task to impart to him the necessary courage and insight to tolerate and master them.'

When Mr Y began psycho-analytical treatment his opening remark to me from the couch was, 'Do you really want me to say everything that comes into my mind?' And when I said 'Yes' he immediately started telling me, with no signs of reserve, the full details of his fantasy life. He kept me, however, almost completely uninformed about the circumstances and events of his everyday life, except for telling me about his studies and his mathematical and philosophical speculations. For a long time these centred round his solution of the problem of solving equations of the fifth degree, a problem which one of his 'fathers' had already proved to be insoluble. As a result he maintained a dissociation between his external life, which was in any case reduced to a minimum by his failure to respond to the overtures of family friends and others who would have been prepared to be hospitable to him, and his fantasy life which he reported to me. His 'hypothetical' defence allowed quite remarkable freedom in fantasy, and he could in imagination roam anywhere. One day we would be in ancient Rome, on another we would be in the eighteenth century, on yet another England would have moved several degrees of latitude south. It also enabled him to gain a considerable sense of being protected by me without his having consciously to admit any sort of attachment. When he visited the dentist, he just happened to have the idea that I was in a room adjoining the surgery; this remained, however, a purely speculative notion; it did not imply that he was anxious and wished me to be around.

Once I had accustomed myself to the fact that he failed to distinguish between different modes of thinking I found no particular difficulty in interpreting the content of his material, which could in general be understood either as deriving from some well-known infantile fantasy or as being the reflection of his denied perception of his real-life predicament. It was often impossible, however, to know whether my interpretations had even been heard, let alone understood. It is after all unnecessary to respond to a hypothetical observation made by a hypothetical analyst on a purely hypothetical notion which just happens to have occurred to one. As a result the analysis continued for many months without my having any feeling that I was communicating with him, and I was deprived of those confirmations and affirmations with which most patients, occasionally at least, reassure us and convince us that our labours are not in vain.

After some time, therefore, I came to the conclusion that the dynamics of the analysis must lie not in understanding the infantile fantasies which his thoughts could be seen to express, but in analysing the defensive function of his whole way of thinking. This could, I concluded, be profitably regarded in three ways.

First, his thoughts were 'cursorily improvised' in the sense that they served the function of filling in the psychic void which had been created by his withdrawal from external objects and the concomitant repression of instinct. In the place of relationships and activities he cathected the process of thinking itself and derived pleasure from passively watching his intellectual processes idling in neutral, as it were. Disengaged from the facts of reality, these intellectual processes could entertain any idea, however anachronistic or bizarre, and bring together notions which reality-testing would have shown to be incompatible. In doing so he produced a simulacrum of the primary process, which could, however, be distinguished from the genuine article by the fact that it aroused neither emotion nor instinct; basically it was unimaginative and purely a matter of verbal manipulation. In fact it exemplified perfectly Freud's description of schizophrenic thinking in his paper 'The Unconscious' (1915). Freud states in this paper that the schizophrenic withdraws cathexis from 'the points which represent the unconscious presentation of the object' while 'the word-presentations corresponding to it . . . receive on the contrary a more intense cathexis'. He adds that this 'cathexis of the word-presentation is not part of the act of repression but represents the first of the attempts at recovery which so conspicuously dominate the clinical picture of schizophrenia'. My patient's 'cursorily improvised' thoughts were in fact part of his attempt to re-create a tolerable world for himself by some means other than that of coming to terms with his primitive impulses.

Secondly, his thinking was a form of masturbation, a playing with his thoughts as a form of self-consolation without, however, ever touching on matters which might have aroused anything dynamic or emotional. It was, in fact, characteristic of his actual masturbation that he always imagined his object to be separated from him by some barrier.

Thirdly, much of his thinking could be regarded as a search for some conception of himself and his place in the world which would restore to him a sense of his significance in some way which would not force him to recognize that he was subject to love, hate, and fear. The only conception which we have of a being who is significant, potent, and yet unperturbable by emotion, is that of God, and much of my patient's thinking could be understood as an attempt to instate himself as God. Philosophically he was a solipsist, and at times he formulated clearly and intelligently the idea that his thoughts were the only reality, and that when he thought, his thoughts were the world in action. This is an idea which only someone who is God can reasonably hold.

Another way in which he tried to make himself godlike was to restrict his conception of reality to his own body; on this view of things the 'world' was his physiology, and the only real events were those which occurred in his alimentary canal, his vascular system, or his brain.

No one who thinks he is God can readily tolerate interference by others, and much of Mr Y's inactivity and withdrawal into a world of sleep and private speculation was an attempt, and in the main a surprisingly successful attempt, to avoid clashes between his universe and those of others, and to avoid situations in which his sense of omnipotence would have been exposed as illusory. On the rare occasions in which he was involved in a clash of wills or felt that someone was prying into his private affairs he showed an arrogant fury that was impressive.

Although Mr Y tried, albeit unsuccessfully, to cure himself by becoming a God who lived in a world of his own creation, the indications were that if he had been successful he would not have been a deity distinguished by benevolence. On the contrary, he appeared to derive considerable satisfaction from contemplating the destruction of millions in the various world wars which he imagined, and the only occasions on which I ever heard him laugh were when he had envisaged some peculiarly horrible and revolting disaster. It was of course this aspect of his pathology which made it impossible for him to identify actively with the father.

Mr Y's defensive system began to break down after three years of analysis, and paranoid fantasies, which had previously been warded off by his seclusion and self-absorption, began to emerge clearly and to influence his behaviour. The first indication of this was his growing conviction that there existed an organization which, for reasons known only to itself, was plotting his death. He never found out who the leaders and members of this organization were, but he nonetheless received intimations of the ways in which they planned to kill him. Sometimes he was to be crucified; at other times he was to be sewn into a sack and thrown into the sea, as had happened to the bishop of his home town in the seventeenth century. It was, he said, terrible to think that in a civilized community people should be allowed to plot such outrages—but he did not entirely despair. The English, he assured himself, are a kind and benevolent people who would never permit such cruelty to occur in their midst. One gathered that he would have been in greater danger nearer home. His sense of being protected so long as he remained in England was sufficiently strong to prevent his ever being seriously disturbed by these ideas. His real complaint was that they pestered him and prevented his concentrating on his studies. The most trying aspect of the organization's activities was its habit of muttering just within earshot that his end was near. In retrospect I am inclined to interpret this fantasy as his distorted perception of the first stirrings of his unconscious.

The next development was more alarming, and caused him to abandon completely not only his private philosophical speculations but also the studies he did at his father's behest, in order to concentrate his powers on the task of resisting a danger which threatened not only himself but the whole of humanity. Two invasions, he believed, were imminent: one was subterranean, while the other, which was the real danger, was to come from outer space.

The subterranean invasion began as an invasion of England by a group of Indians and Italians who tunnelled under the English Channel and then proceeded northwards. On reaching London they headed for the neighbourhood in which he lived, and on occasion he saw individual members of the invading force reconnoitring above ground. Although Mr Y viewed this invasion with certain misgivings, he regularly praised the Italians and Indians and expressed admiration for their intelligence and courage. He also at the same time had the idea that General Eisenhower, who had become one of his 'fathers', was busy building a tunnel connecting my consulting room with his lodgings. This fact and his general attitude towards this subterranean invasion, made me believe that the fantasy was in essentials benign and progressive, and that it represented the emergence from repression of his own drives and capacities. Once when I made an interpretation to this effect he told me that the previous evening he had seen himself standing in the shadow a short distance from his lodgings.

The invasion from outer space, on the other hand, was unequivocally bad, and consisted of a force of beings whose sole aim was to destroy the whole universe known to man. He appeared to give them no concrete image; they were quite simply evil and aggression incarnate. Individual members of an advance force who appeared in London's parks, however, were disguised as dwarfs.

This delusional fantasy had, I think, three meanings. First, it represented Mr Y's own primitive aggression, which he denied and projected and which therefore presented itself to him as something totally alien and inhuman. It was a manifestation of *the return of the repressed,* and not the emergence of unconscious forces from repression in a way that he could assimilate. Secondly, it represented his presentiment that as his drives and unconscious fantasies returned from repression he would be faced with a clash between his own private, distorted sense of reality and that of others, a clash which could, he felt, only end in the annihilation either of his world or of that of everyone else. As his response to the expected invasion was to design and construct a hydrogen bomb, which would itself, he believed, be capable of destroying the whole world, he was clearly identified as much with the invaders as with the universe they were going to destroy. Thirdly, the invasion referred to the imminent visit to this country of his eighteen-year-old younger brother, who personified for him some of the most threatening and unacceptable aspects of the external world, and who was in his own way quite as narcissistic and impenetrable as Mr Y himself.

As the invasion from outer space became nearer, Mr Y became increasingly agitated and devoted himself to his project of constructing an atomic bomb which would save the world from the evil that was threatening it. Mr Y was a scientific, intellectual Saviour, and when he renounced the quiet of his studies to save mankind it was to use his intellectual powers to resist an *external* danger which threatened humanity. He shared with his more psychologically minded predecessors, however, the expectation, which was indeed realized, that he would have to work without recognition and that he would be subjected to scorn, mockery, and humiliation. In fact the bomb was a pathetic contraption, improvised out of lead piping, ball-bearings, and wire, and only in its creator's imagination could it be conceived to have any function at all. The theoretical principles underlying its design were laid out in a mathematical argument which he brought to the analysis, while the bomb itself was proudly displayed to his landlady, who watched its growth with the sympathetic indulgence that she would have given to something a child of her own was making out of Meccano.

It was at this point, when the patient stopped concealing the extent of his illness by restricting his fantastic activity to thought and instead began to *do* things for which he sought the interest and approval of others, that the analysis began to get out of hand. Previously, it had proceeded in the security of a social vacuum. Mr Y lived several hundred miles from his family and had rejected every social contact he had been offered in London, his landlady tolerated his eccentric behaviour, enjoyed his dependence on her, and protected him from the intrustions of external reality, while his analyst conformed strictly to the convention of non-interference. In retrospect I regret that I had at this time no appreciation of the extent to which Mr Y was satisfying his widowed landlady's wish to have another child, and had therefore no inkling of the lengths to which she was prepared to go to suppress and deny facts which would have suggested that her adopted child would have been better in hospital. When, as happened shortly before his admission to hospital, I saw them together, I was very touched by her simple and direct approach to him and by his absolute trust in her, but realized that her ability to respond so completely to him was dependent on the fact that she regarded him solely as a child and not at all as a childish adult. As a result she was uninhibited by any feeling that he cut a tragic figure, but blind to any of his potential assets. Whether her love for him was absolutely contingent on his remaining ill, and whether, if so, he sensed this, I do not know. The point I wish to make here, however, is that my patient and she colluded to form a *folie à deux* by which *he* was able to act out his fantasies within an environment in which they were protected from reality-testing, and *she* found an outlet for unsatisfied maternal impulses, and that this world of illusion, so far from being a setting in which my patient could find his feet imaginatively, as it would have been if he had actually been a child, became in fact a fool's paradise, from which he was bound eventually to be expelled.

That Mr Y's invasion-fantasies represented the emergence of true unconscious forces and were not merely manipulations of verbal presentations was shown by the fact that they were accompanied by intense anxiety, similar, it can be presumed, to that which he had suffered as an adolescent. He turned again to drugs and started eating the contents of benedrex inhalers.

At the end of July 1959 his young brother arrived in England. This brother, whom I saw once, seemed quite incapable of appreciating how ill the patient was and my advice that he should handle him gently. Instead he treated him as though he were not ill at all, and made no attempt to conceal his contempt for his brother's contraption. As a result Mr Y found that

his bomb, which had previously only been the subject of interpretation by myself and of indulgent interest by his landlady,
had suddenly become an object of mockery, and that he himself had become the butt of his brother's sarcastic humour. An
open clash occurred, therefore, between his psychical reality
and that of another, and, instead of being able to live in an
illusory world where he felt himself to be a person of some consequence, he was compelled to face the fact that in his brother's
eyes he was ridiculous, pathetic, and impotent. His reaction to
this clash of worlds was mounting anger and tension, increased
consumption of amphetamine, and, finally, self-protective
action; he started to carry a hammer with which to defend
himself not only against invaders from outer space but also
from those in this world who threatened him. At this point
those around him very understandably took fright, and it
became necessary to commit him to hospital; this I myself did.
As Mr Y shook hands with me before getting into the ambu-
lance, he pointed upwards and said, 'Look, Dr Rycroft, there
are two moons in the sky tonight.' This I took to mean that he
had decided to recognize the existence of two realities, one by
which others live and to which he must outwardly conform, and
another which he must keep to himself. The solution of splitting,
by which the derivatives of infantile omnipotent fantasies
and the concomitant grandiose, solipsistic conception of the self
are contained within a delusional system which is dissociated
from that part of the self which handles external relations, was
also that adopted by Schreber. Although Schreber continued
to believe that he was a Redeemer and God's Spouse, he never
tried to impose this conception of himself on others, and only
in strictest privacy did he ever indulge his notion that he was a
woman. 'I have now been long aware,' he wrote several years
after his recovery, 'that the persons I see about me are not
cursorily improvised men but real people, and that I must
therefore behave towards them as a reasonable man is used to
behave towards his fellows.'

Six months after his admission to hospital Mr Y came to see
me. Only for a moment did our conversation get beyond
trivialities. This was when I asked him whether he was still
interested in mathematics. 'Inventing things, you mean?' he
said, and I agreed that this was indeed what I had meant.

'Oh no, I've given that up completely' and then after a long pause and with a broad grin ' . . . for the present, anyhow.'

My original purpose in writing this paper was to attempt an imaginative reconstruction of the inner experience of someone who has come to regard external reality as 'hypothetical' or 'cursorily improvised', and for whom experience has ceased to have any value. But as the paper wrote itself I realized that I was in fact suggesting an interpretation of the schizophrenic's relation to his perceptions which differed in some respects from that made by Freud in his paper on Schreber. There, as I have already mentioned, Freud interprets Schreber's description of the world as being peopled by 'cursorily improvised' men as the consequence of his having withdrawn cathexis from external reality. This, however, cannot be the end of the matter, since this interpretation (*a*) leaves unanswered the question 'By whom were they cursorily contrived?' and (*b*) fails to explain why 'cursorily improvised' men should also be 'magically conjured-up', a phrase which suggests that they must have been products of Schreber's omnipotence. This is one reason why I have stressed the solipsistic implications of my patient's material. But the contradiction which appears to exist between the ideas of cursory improvisation and magical conjuring-up can, I believe, be resolved if one views the patient's relation to his thought-processes historically. Mr Y's illness began with a process which can be described either as a withdrawal of cathexis from external objects or as a withdrawal of cathexis, following massive repression, from 'the points which represent the unconscious presentations' of external objects. As a result of this withdrawal external reality ceased to have any meaning for him, and he ceased to have any relationships which gave him any sense of significance. He could derive this neither from external objects nor from any belief in his own instinctual capacities; he had cut himself off from both by the same defence, which gave him freedom from guilt and anxiety at the cost of becoming a nonentity in his own eyes, a person with no roots either within or without. During this phase of his illness his thoughts were cursorily improvised in the sense that they lacked that force and solidity which only adheres to thoughts which derive from an instinctual interest in real objects. Life in this state must be one of maximal despair, disillusion, and futility, and the spontaneous attempts at recovery, which, as Freud showed, play such a conspicuous part in the symptomatology of schizophrenia, must be regarded as attempts to escape from this state of nonentity by some route other than that of insight into the nature of what has been repressed. The attempts at recovery are in fact a defence, designed to protect the patient from either re-experiencing despair or recognizing the strength and nature of his impulses. This defence is, in the widest sense of the term, 'manic'. It involves denial of psychical reality and omnipotent reversal of the true psychical situation; the thoughts which in psychical truth have become bereft of significance come to be regarded as precisely the only objects to have any significance. The sole survivors of the psychic catastrophe of repression come to be regarded as the only inhabitants the world has ever had. The stones which the builder rejected become the foundations of a self-fabricated world. Once this omnipotent reversal has occurred, the cursorily improvised becomes the magically conjured-up, and the way is open to creating a new world in which a new significance and a new identity can be found—or rather could be, were it not for the presence of other human beings in the external world which the patient must perforce continue to inhabit. It is at this point in the process of the so-called 'recovery' that the falsity of the omnipotent defence becomes apparent. It is useless to become God, or God's spouse, or even a Margrave of Tuscany and Tasmania, if such a self-estimation is ignored by all those on whom the patient depends for his continued survival. He has then no choice but to compromise. He must either live such a secluded life that his omnipotent fantasies never clash with the reality-conceptions of others, or he must modify his ideas so that they gain him disciples; or must, as Schreber did, keep his private fantasies to himself and learn to behave towards others 'as a reasonable man is used to behave towards his fellows'. This last compromise was reached by my patient when he declared that there were two moons in the sky.

8

Beyond the Reality Principle[1]

1. There are two types, modes or forms of mental functioning.

2. Under conditions of 'ideal' or 'normal' mental health these are integrated and analysis of the totality of mental activity into discrete types of function is impossible.

3. In all forms of mental ill-health, however, dissociation occurs and the specific characteristics of both types of mental functioning become observable.

'A complete divergence of their trends, a total severance of the two systems, is what above all characterizes a condition of illness.' (Freud, 1915, p. 194.)

4. These two types of mental functioning were called by Freud the primary and secondary processes, which he conceived as being actuated by the pleasure and reality principles. According to Freud the primary processes precede the secondary in individual development and are or become unconscious, while the secondary processes arise as a result of growth and experience of external reality and are conscious. He also held that the primary processes have an intrinsic connexion with dream imagery ('thing-representations'), fantasy, and wish-fulfilling hallucinatory tendencies, and the secondary processes with verbal imagery ('word-representations') and 'reality-adaptation'.

5. The notion that the primary processes precede the secondary in individual development has frequently been questioned, and on one occasion Freud himself described it as a fiction.

It will rightly be objected that an organization which was a slave to the pleasure-principle and neglected the reality of the external world could not maintain itself alive for the shortest time, so that it could not come into existence at all. The employment of a fiction like this is, however, justified when one considers that

---

[1] First published in the *Int. J. Psycho-Anal.* (1962), **43.**

the infant—provided that one includes with it the care it receives from its mother—does almost realize a psychical system of this kind (Freud, 1911*b*, p.220. fn.).

This quotation shows that Freud's notion that the primary processes precede the secondary in individual development was dependent on his having been impressed by the helplessness of the infant and his having therefore assumed that the mother-infant relationship, which he would appear never to have studied in detail, was one in which the mother was active and the infant totally passive, in which the mother was in touch with reality while the infant only had wishes. If, however, one starts from the assumption that the mother is the infant's external reality and that the mother–infant relationship is from the very beginning a process of mutual adaptation, to which the infant contributes by actions such as crying, clinging, and sucking, which evoke maternal responses in the mother, one is forced to conclude that the infant engages in realistic and adaptive be-haviour, that the secondary processes operate coevally with the primary, and that ego-functions cannot initially be differen-tiated from instinctual discharges.

The idea that, given adequate mothering, situations occur recurrently in an infant's life in which his (presumed) hallucina-tions are realized occupies a central position in Winnicott's work on the nature of illusion and its function in infantile development (Winnicott, 1958). It has also been discussed by Milner (1952) and by myself (Chapters III and IV of the present volume).

6. The notion that the secondary processes are solely the result of experience of external reality is not only incompatible with the biological and ethological evidence in favour of the ex-istence of innate adaptive responses (cf. Bowlby, 1958, 1960*a*, *b*), but also raises insoluble problems of ontogeny. When in his lecture 'The Anatomy of the Mental Personality' (1933) Freud describes the id, which is clearly the topographical equivalent of the primary processes, as a chaos with no organization and then goes on to describe the ego as 'that part of the id which has been modified by its proximity to the external world', he poses conundrums about the origin of the ego—e. g. in what way can a chaos experience the external world in such a way as to be organized by it?—which do not arise if one starts from the assumption of primary integration and regards maturation as

proceeding not from chaos to organization but from simple to complex forms of organization.

7. The notion that the primary processes are necessarily unconscious is untenable since

(*a*) dreams are conscious;

(*b*) the conscious operation of the primary processes can be observed in (i) various pathological phenomena, notably hysterical dissociated states and fetishistic activity, and (ii) imaginative activity such as play in children and artistic creation in adults. (In this paragraph, as elsewhere in this communication, I have used the word 'unconscious' in its descriptive, phenomenological sense and not in its theoretical sense of 'appertaining to the system Ucs'. In classical psycho-analytical theory it is entirely legitimate to refer to a remembered dream as a conscious manifestation of the system Ucs, but to do so in the present context would be to beg the very question under discussion.)

8. The intrinsic connexion between the secondary processes and verbal imagery, and between the primary processes and dream imagery, is better stated by saying that the symbolism of the secondary processes is discursive and that of the primary is non-discursive. Susanne Langer (1942) describes non-discursive symbolism as a mode of mental activity which uses visual and auditory imagery rather than words, which presents its constituents simultaneously and not successively, which operates imaginatively (e.g. 'to conceive prospective changes in familiar scenes') but is incapable of generalizing, which has no grammar or syntax, and which uses elements that derive their meaning from their relations to the other symbols simultaneously present and not from any defined or dictionary meaning. Discursive symbolism on the other hand is the symbolism of conscious rational thinking, in which words are presented successively according to the conventions of grammar, syntax, and dictionary.

9. Correlation of the primary processes with non-discursive symbolism makes it possible to ascribe to them a function, that of expression, explication, and communication of the feeling attaching to experience, in contrast to the function of the secondary processes, which is to analyse external reality into discrete elements, to categorize them and formulate statements about the relations existing between them.

10. The notion that the primary processes are necessarily unconscious derives from the assumptions

(*a*) that they lack function and must therefore be rendered inoperative if adaptation is to occur;

(*b*) that repression is the primary defence mechanism.

11. Assumption (*a*) falls to the ground once a function can be assigned. The notion that the primary processes are concerned solely with fantasies of an 'unrealistic' and 'non-adaptive' kind ignores the part played in full adaptation by affects and imagination, and by the need to express and communicate them. The thesis presented here is that the secondary processes are 'realistic' when they are used to relate to the external world objectively, while the primary processes are 'realistic' when they are used to relate affectively to objects of emotional interest. The secondary processes, then, are the form of mental activity which corresponds to the self-preservative component of adaptation, while the primary processes are the form of mental activity which corresponds to the libidinal component of adaptation. Dissociated application of the secondary processes to affective relationships is unrealistic and non-adaptive —clinically it presents as 'intellectual defence'; so too is dissociated application of the primary processes to the nature of external reality, which presents as pre-logical, animistic thinking.

12. The notion that repression is the primary defence mechanism is not in accord either with most recent psycho-analytical research, which tends to assign priority to splitting and projection (cf. Klein and Fairbairn), nor with Freud's own view that denial, followed by projection, is the original defence against pain. Denial, splitting, and projection do not necessarily render the affected psychic processes unconscious, though they do render them alien and 'not self'. Repression is to be regarded as one possible vicissitude of a denied, split-off mental process (cf. Madison, 1956).

13. Scientific thinking requires the capacity to dissociate mental activity in such a way that the secondary processes can operate undisturbed by the primary processes. This dissociation may be either free, in which case it is an adaptive mechanism, or compulsive, in which case it is a defence mechanism. When operating freely its function is to enable the relationships existing between objects and processes occurring in external reality to be perceived and conceptualized without interference from emotional bias and animistic thinking, and to test the validity

of hypotheses which have been arrived at imaginatively. When operating compulsively its defensive function is to protect the individual from the irruption of dissociated fantasies.

14. Since psycho-analysis aims at being a scientific psychology, psycho-analytical observation and theorizing is involved in the paradoxical activity of using secondary process thinking to observe, analyse, and conceptualize precisely that form of mental activity, the primary processes, which scientific thinking has always been at pains to exclude.

> Around the year 500 B.C. natural science began with a repudiation of the dream. Heracleitos of Ephesos issued a scientific manifesto in the two sentences 'We must not act and speak like sleepers, for in our sleep too we act and speak' and 'The waking have one world in common, but the sleeping turn aside each into a world of his own' . . . at the very dawn of science the dream and the psychologic symptoms were such nuisances that science could not begin until they were explicitly expelled from scientific consideration (Lewin, 1958, pp 11–12).

From this derives the tendency of classical analytical theory to conceptualize primary process mentation, fantasy, and often even emotion, in terms which suggest that tney have an intrinsic tendency to be experienced as alien and intrusive to the self, to describe the primary processes as primitive, archaic, unrealistic, etc., and to treat artistic and religious phenomena as analogues of neurosis. In other words, the observing and operative self, the ego in Freud's terminology, has been cast in the mould of the scientist at work, and the normal man implied by theory has been modelled on the rationalist ideal. But, since

(i) the basic discovery made by psycho-analysis has been the ubiquity of 'irrational' primary process activity in human psychic life;

(ii) psycho-analytical theory constitutes an attempt to describe primary process thinking in the language of the secondary processes; and

(iii) psycho-analytical treatment comprises a technique for making dissociated and repressed mental processes available to the self, the tendency of psycho-analysis is to create a conception of human personality which *includes* just those elements which its original assumed ego *excludes*. It is this paradox which explains the tortuosities in which ego-psychology becomes involved when it attempts to describe affective processes in a way that evaluates them positively.

From the point of view of the psychology of the neuroses, affective action—in contrast to the theoretical ideal of rational action— often appears as a deplorable residue of primitive mental conditions and as a deviation from the normal. We see much more clearly that affective action gives rise to therapeutic difficulties than that it also gives an impetus for mastering reality. Yet we do know the crucial rôle of affectivity in organizing and facilitating many ego functions; Freud (1937) implied this when he said that analysis is not expected to free man of all passions (Hartmann, 1939).

It is possible, and even probable, that it is just this sharper differentiation of the ego and the id—the more precise division of labour between them—in human adults (as compared to animals) which on the one hand makes for a superior, more flexible, relation to the external world, and on the other increases the *alienation of the id from reality (ibid.*, Hartmann's italics.)

These quotations show clearly that the theoretical ideal of rational action predicated by ego-psychology alienates the human adult from the springs of emotion, even though it cannot be expected to free him entirely from all passions. Small wonder that it was a psycho-analyst who produced the aphorism 'We are born mad, acquire morality, and become stupid and unhappy. Then we die.' (Eder, 1932.)

Rather similarly, the obscurity into which Hartmann falls when he writes about art and religion seems to derive from the fact that, although he sees clearly that their function is—or can be—synthesizing and integrative, his view that their origins are in an archaic layer of the mind which is alien to the ego compels him to resort to dualistic concepts such as 'regressive adaptation' and 'detour through the archaic' to account for them (Hartmann, 1939, pp. 77–9).

'The attempt to understand Freud, as well as Hartmann and other contemporary Freudians, presents the endlessly fascinating and difficult problem of trying to distinguish meaning from words, of trying to discern the central thrust of the thought of a creative person through the images and metaphors of his time in which he has almost inevitably expressed it. The same problem appears in a very different form in, for example, the attempt to enter into the meaning of George Herbert and the other metaphysical poets of the seventeenth century. They used the symbolism of the liturgy and the religious art of their time; but in using it they both enlarged the meaning of the symbols and used the symbols to enlarge their vision of the meaning of life. In reading Freud it is not easy to know when the metaphors and analogies that were those of his time constricted his thought' (Lynd, 1958).

This comparison of Lynd's acquires added point when one remembers that historians date the rise of the scientific outlook and method from the seventeenth century (cf. Hull, 1959, Ch. 7) and that since then there has been a 'dissociation of sensibility' (Eliot, 1921) as a result of which modern man, unlike medieval man, views reality from two unconnected and incompatible standpoints, one scientific and objective, the other imaginative and subjective. The problem of understanding Freud, to which Lynd refers, derives in part from his having been compelled, as a scientist, to use language which presupposes this split to express ideas which annul it.

15. If the notion that the primary processes are archaic, unrealistic, and inherently non-adaptive is discarded, it becomes necessary to explain why the scientific mode of thinking, when applied to the psychological field, encounters phenomena which it tends to conceive in terms antithetical to itself, which it readily envisages to be not only antithetical but also antagonistic, and which it is therefore predisposed to describe in pejorative and negative terms.

> You must not expect me to tell you much that is new about the id, except its name. It is the obscure inaccessible part of our personality; the little we know about it we have learnt from the study of dream-work and the formation of neurotic symptoms, and most of that is of a negative character, and can only be described as being all that the ego is not. We come nearer to the id with images, and call it a chaos, a cauldron of seething excitement. (Freud, 1933, p. xxxi.)

16. The explanation has already been foreshadowed in the preceding paragraphs, where it has been suggested

(a) that dissociation of psychic functioning into two types or modes, one objective, the other animistic and affective (is a defence which) occurs in all types of mental dysfunction—'a total severance of the two systems is what above all characterizes a condition of illness.'

(*b*) that this dissociation has been creatively exploited by Western intellectuals to produce the scientific attitude and method, but

(*c*) that application of this attitude to the field of psychology has turned out to be a paradoxical activity, inasmuch as it has necessitated calling into question the nature of the ego, the very entity which the classical scientific attitude takes for granted. Psycho-analytical research, therefore, poses problems relating (i) to the pathology of the Western intellectual tradition, and (ii) to the status of the observer in scientific work.

17. The relationship established between the primary and secondary processes in any particular individual depends on

(*a*) quantitative factors, such as the extent of the dissociation. If nearly total, the individual is alienated from his emotional, imaginative, and intuitive functions and lacks understanding of the 'logic of emotions'. If confined to certain, circumscribed aspects of mental life, he senses no disharmony between his intellectual and imaginative functions except in the particular areas affected by the dissociation;

(*b*) the mechanisms used to deal with the consequences of the dissociation. If repression is used, the individual will be unaware of his loss of primary process capacity except when, and insofar as, the repression is breaking down (the return of the repressed). When this occurs he will develop symptoms and become aware of the working within himself of some force by which he feels threatened. Similar effects will ensue when mechanisms which reinforce repression (e.g. reaction-formation) are used. On the other hand, the individual who does not use repression (or whose repressive defences have collapsed) and whose split is unburied, will be aware of the presence either in himself or in someone (or -thing) else, with whom he is obsessed, of fantasies drives, etc., from which he feels alienated and by which he feels threatened;

(*c*) which process has acquired dominance over the other. Hartmann's 'theoretical ideal of rational action' presupposes that in normal development the secondary processes became dominant over the primary, and Freud made the same assumption when he compared the relationship between the ego and the id to that of a rider and his horse.

> The horse provides the locomotive energy, and the rider has the prerogative of determining the goal and of guiding the movements of his powerful mount towards it. But all too often in the relations between the ego and the id we find a picture of the less ideal situation in which the rider is obliged to guide his horse in the direction in which it itself wishes to go. (Freud, 1933, p. xxxi.)

Since, however, human beings are single creatures and not phantom psyches mounted on an animal body, this metaphor, which neatly describes the state of affairs existing in psychoneurotics, presupposes as normal a split between mind and body, between will and desire, which can itself be regarded as pathological. We have to be able to envisage, though this too may be a 'theoretical ideal', the person for whom the opposition assumed by this metaphor is not valid, i.e. the integrated person as opposed to the controlled one, the person whose health is a primary psychobiological phenomenon and not a 'secondary construction'.

The fact that relationships can exist between the secondary and primary processes other than (successful or unsuccessful) dominance of the latter by the former is shown by

(*a*) schizophrenic thinking, in which the secondary process function of thinking with verbal images is taken over by the primary processes in such a way that the patient uses the apparatus of factual statement to make condensed, cryptic utterances about his affective state, so that what is really poetic expression of his inner life presents as nonsensical prose and

(*b*) the existence of persons who have the capacity to perform what ego-psychology calls 'regressions in the service of the ego' (Kris, 1934, quoted by Hartmann, *op. cit.*)

> Nor will it be out of place here to utter a warning against any over-hasty generalization of what we have brought to light concerning the distribution of the various mental functions between the two systems. We are describing the state of affairs as it appears in the adult human being, in whom the systems *Ucs* operates, strictly speaking, only as a preliminary stage of the higher organization. The question of what the content and con-

nexions of that system are during the development of the individual, and of what significance it possesses in animals—these are points on which no conclusion can be deduced from our description: they must be investigated independently. Moreover, in human beings we must be prepared to find possible pathological conditions under which the two systems alter, or even exchange, both their content and their characteristics. (Freud, 1915, p. 189).

18. Insofar, then, as dissociation between the primary processes and the secondary processes does not occur, fantasy continues to engage external reality (objects), enriches it, and enables the imaginative elaborations of personal relationships to be understood and appreciated. Fantasy remains 'egotized' in that

(*a*) its activities are felt to be an essential part of the self, to be 'ego-syntonic', and

(*b*) it performs an adaptive function, viz., that of preventing the boredom (*acedia*) which ensues if ego-development is the result of passive, forced adaptation. Insofar, however, as dissociation does occur, fantasy becomes disengaged from external reality (objects), emotional appreciation of which is impoverished, and becomes an activity from which the individual feels alienated.

19. Disengagement of fantasy is responsible for the chaotic and bizarre impression created by the primary processes of the mentally ill, since under conditions of dissociation the condensing tendency of the primary processes leads to substitutions and equations of mental images that are unrelated to the actual nature and function of the objects represented. When fantasy does engage reality, this same process, condensation, leads to perception of similarities and to understanding of symbolic communication (cf. Jones, 1916, Section III).

20. Disengagement is also responsible for the infantile content of neurotic fantasy, since the resulting isolation from experience prevents maturation.

21. In place, therefore, of the hypothesis that psychic development proceeds by repression of an innate tendency to hallucinatory wish-fulfilment and superimposition of a learned capacity for adaptation, the alternative hypothesis is suggested that the human infant begins life in a state of primary integration in which his expectations (i.e. his capacity to imagine objects providing satisfaction) and his capacity to perceive and

signal are in line with one other and both correspond to the possible responses of what Hartmann has called 'an average expectable environment' and Winnicott has called 'an ordinary devoted mother'. Insofar as his expectations are fulfilled, primary integration continues and he retains the feeling of primary relatedness to the environment; he feels at home in the world and his fantasies remain bound to external objects. Insofar, however, as expectations are disappointed and the state of primary relatedness is disrupted, dissociation occurs in such a way that wishful thinking and adaptive adjustment come to operate in different psychic realms. Imaginative capacity becomes disengaged from external reality and operates in a psychic realm in which images cease to *represent* external objects and become instead *substitutes* for them (cf. Segal, 1957; also my paper on symbolism—Chapter 4 in the present volume).

The various clinical categories with which we are familiar arise from differences

(*a*) in the intensity of the disruption of the stage of primary relatedness, and the age at which it occurs (i.e. in the nature, extent, and timing of the disillusion);

(*b*) in the relative distribution of libidinal and aggressive drives within the psychic realms of inner and outer reality, and

(*c*) in the mechanisms used to establish equilibrium between the divided psychic tendencies.

Hysterics who repress their aggressive feelings but permit free expression of their libidinal wishes on the condition that this occurs solely within the realm of dissociated fantasy, display the state of affairs most nearly exemplifying the classical formulation of the relationship between the primary and secondary processes; libidinal satisfaction is provided by wish-fulfilling fantasy and hallucination, adaptation is a learned process felt to be antagonistic to satisfaction. What is omitted from the classical formulation is the hysteric's hatred of external objects arising from their supposed intrinsically frustrating and rejecting nature. According to the hypothesis being presented here this hatred is a consequence of the disruption of the state of primary relatedness and is a symptom of the resulting alienation. (For further evidence that hate results from disruption of states of relatedness see the evidence collected by Bowlby showing how frequently bereavement is followed by aggressive outbursts (Bowlby, 1960*a*, *b*; also Lindemann, 1944).

22. If the hypothesis presented here is correct, the aim of psycho-analytical treatment is not primarily to make the unconscious conscious, nor to widen or strengthen the ego, but to re-establish the connexion between dissociated psychic functions, so that the patient ceases to feel that there is an inherent antagonism between his imaginative and adaptive capacities.

Only connect the prose and the passion . . . and both will be exalted, and human love will be seen at its height. Live in fragments no longer. Only connect, and the beast and the monk, robbed of the isolation that is life to either, will die. (Forster, 1910, Chap. xii.)

The essential note in the new sensibility is actually the determination never in any way to forget that spiritual or cultural functions are equally and simultaneously biological functions. Further, that culture for that reason cannot be exclusively directed by its objective laws, or laws independent of life, but is at the same time subject to the laws of life. We are governed by two contrasted imperatives. Man as a living being must be good, orders the one, the cultural imperative: What is good must be human, must be lived and so compatible with and necessary to life, says the other imperative, the vital one. Giving a more generic expression to both, we shall reach the conception of the double mandate, life must be cultured, but culture is bound to be vital. We are dealing, then, with two kinds of pressure, which mutually regulate and modify one another. Any fault in equilibrium in favour of one or the other involves, irremediably, a degeneration. Uncultured life is barbarism, devitalized culture is Byzantinism . . . Culture, or reason, has been refined to the last degree, almost to the point of severance from spontaneous life, which, for its own part, has remained equally isolated but in a crude and practically aboriginal state. This condition of extreme tension inaugurated the unique dynamic quality, the endless vicissitudes and the permanent restlessness of the history of this continent. (Ortega y Gasset, 1931.)

9

The Analysis of a Detective Story[1]

Of the various psycho-analysts who have discussed the psychology of the detective story only one, Geraldine Pedersen-Krag, has put forward a specific hypothesis to account for their popularity. In her article 'Detective Stories and the Primal Scene' (1949) she suggests that it arises from their ability to re-awaken the interest and curiosity originally aroused by observation of the primal scene. According to her the murder is a symbolic representation of parental intercourse and

> the victim is the parent for whom the reader (the child) had negative oedipal feelings. The clues in the story, disconnected, inexplicable and trifling, represent the child's growing awareness of details it had never understood, such as the family sleeping arrangements, nocturnal sounds, stains, incomprehensible adult jokes and remarks . . . The reader addicted to mystery stories tries actively to relive and master traumatic infantile experiences he once had to endure passively. Becoming the detective, he gratifies his infantile curiosity with impunity, redressing completely the helpless inadequacy and anxious guilt unconsciously remembered from childhood.

It is possible to draw a deduction from this hypothesis which Pedersen-Krag does not herself explicitly make. If the victim is the parent for whom the reader (the child) had negative oedipal feelings, then the criminal must be a personification of the reader's own unavowed hostility towards that parent. The reader is not only the detective; he is also the criminal. One reason, I suspect, why the detective story so rarely achieves the status of a work of art is that this identification of the reader with the criminal remains denied. The detective story writer connives with the reader's need to deny his guilt by providing

[1] Read before the London Imago Group, 21 February 1956, and the British Psycho-Analytical Society, 16 May 1956; and first published in the *Psychoanal. Quart.* (1957), **26**.

him with ready-made fantasies in which the compulsive question 'whodunnit?' is always answered by a self-exonerating 'not I'. In the ideal detective story the detective or hero would discover that he himself is the criminal for whom he has been seeking. Such a story, though it is not generally accounted a detective story, does in fact exist and has given its name to the very psychological constellation which endows observations and fantasies of the primal scene with such significance. I am referring, of course, to the myth of Oedipus, the cathartic effect of which depends on the fact that the guilt, which the typical detective story denies, is openly admitted. Another way of putting the point I am making here is to say that reading detective stories is in a way the opposite of having psycho-analytical treatment. The motive underlying one is to deny insight and underlying the other is to gain it.

Pedersen-Krag brings forward a number of general considerations in support of her suggestion. She mentions, for instance, the close connexion existing between curiosity and its inhibition and the trauma of witnessing the primal scene, and draws a parallel between the voyeur's inability ever to be satisfied with his peeping and the detective story addict's compulsion to read endless variations of the same basic mystery tale. She does not, however, produce either of the two specific types of evidence that are really necessary to validate her hypothesis. She does not present any clinical material tending to show that compulsive readers or writers of detective stories display any of the symptoms or character-problems that one might expect to encounter in persons for whom observation of the primal scene had been a specific pathogenic experience, e.g. anxiety-ridden curiosity, pathological jealousy, a compulsive need to control their objects or a tendency to use projective mechanisms as a defence against depression. Nor does she attempt the analysis of any particular detective story in order to show in detail that it contains a disguised, symbolic representation of the primal scene.

I should remark here in parenthesis that Pedersen-Krag's hypothesis is that the detective story addict is attempting to master a traumatic experience by, as she puts it, reliving actively what once had to be endured passively, whereas I should myself be inclined to say that he is living a fantasy of being in omnipotent control of the internalised parents. For her, reading detective stories is analogous to a traumatic neurosis, whereas I conceive it as a form of manic defence and am sceptical as to the necessity to assume any actual traumatic observation of the primal scene. It will be appreciated that this difference in formulation stems from theoretical considerations which are rather remote from the specific theme of this paper.

In respect of the first of Pedersen-Krag's omissions I have nothing to contribute myself, as I have as yet never encountered a patient with any particular interest in detective fiction; nor have I myself. In respect of the second, however, I should like to present an analysis of a very well-known detective novel which to my mind confirms in a very obvious and indeed surprising way at least part of Pedersen-Krag's hypothesis and which has a number of other features which make it of sufficient interest to be the subject of a paper.

When I say that it confirms part of Pedersen-Krag's hypothesis, I mean that to my mind the crime on which this novel centres very obviously represents a sexual intercourse but that only theoretical constructions of a rather complex and less immediately convincing nature justify one in assuming that the intercourse in question is the primal scene. On the face of it, indeed, it represents an intercourse of a rather different kind, one which has, however, itself a quite special psychological significance.

Wilkie Collins's novel, *The Moonstone*, was published in 1868 and was the first full-length detective story ever to be written in English. Its only precursors are three short stories by Edgar Allan Poe written in the 1840s (cf. Bonaparte, 1933) and one detective novel in French, Emile Gaboriau's *L'Affaire Lerouge*, which was published in 1866. In the opinion of both T. S. Eliot and Dorothy Sayers *The Moonstone* remains the finest detective story in the English language. As perhaps befits the progenitor of a literary line that has displayed such vitality it is considerably longer than most of its modern descendants and has an even more complicated plot. In summarizing it I shall therefore be fairly ruthless in my elimination of themes that seem to me to be irrelevant to the main points that I wish to make. I shall also confine myself, so far as is possible, to those parts and details of the story, the symbolic and unconscious meaning of which will be immediately apparent to those who are accustomed to listening with the third ear, and shall omit various aspects of the story which could only be interpreted after lengthy and rather speculative theoretical argument.

Since writing the first draft of this paper I have discovered that two of the major themes that I have eliminated in this summary were also omitted by Wilkie Collins when he prepared a dramatic version of *The Moonstone*. It is generally agreed that by doing so he completely destroyed whatever literary merit the original novel had. It seems to me that this fact has in it somewhere a moral for the psycho-analyst who wishes to turn literary critic.

The central crime of *The Moonstone* is not a murder but a theft. Rachel Verinder, a young heiress, has been bequeathed a diamond by her uncle with the express condition that it be presented to her in person on her eighteenth birthday. The diamond is of exceptional size and beauty and its perfection is only marred by a central flaw. It is called the Moonstone on account of its having the property of 'growing and lessening in lustre with the waxing and waning of the moon'. The task of handing the diamond over to Rachel falls to her cousin, Franklin Blake, who pays an extended visit to her home during the weeks immediately prior to her eighteenth birthday. Franklin and Rachel fall in love. On her eighteenth birthday Rachel is given the Moonstone and she wears it at the dinner-party given in her honour. After the guests have departed and she is about to go to bed her mother entreats Rachel to give her the diamond for safe-keeping. Rachel refuses and asserts her independence by insisting that she will put the diamond in an unlocked drawer of an Indian cabinet in her sitting-room, which immediately adjoins her bedroom. She dismisses her mother's protests with a contemptuous 'Good heavens, Mamma! Is this an hotel? Are there thieves in the house?'

Next morning the Moonstone has disappeared. Sergeant Cuff of Scotland Yard is soon called in and he shows that the essential clue is that the garment worn by the thief must have on it a stain of paint off Rachel's sitting-room door, on which Franklin and Rachel have been doing 'decorative painting' together. The colour of the paint is not mentioned. It emerges later that the garment in question is a man's nightshirt.

After the theft is discovered Rachel shuts herself in her room and refuses to speak to anyone, but it soon becomes obvious by her behaviour that she is convinced that she knows who stole the Moonstone. Later it becomes apparent that she has the best of reasons for her conviction, since she actually saw the Moonstone being taken. At the end of the novel one realizes that its whole mystery and suspense stem from two apparently inexplicable omissions on Rachel's part. She fails to interrupt the thief and she refuses to respond to her mother's entreaties that she tell her what she knows about the crime.

After the disappearance of the Moonstone Franklin is foremost in taking steps to discover the thief and it is he who calls in Sergeant Cuff after the local police have shown themselves incompetent to handle the case. At first he cannot understand why his efforts evoke an intensely hostile response from Rachel, but eventually he realizes that she believes him to be the thief. He is therefore appalled to discover that increasingly the evidence does in fact point towards himself as the criminal. He himself discovers the missing garment and finds that it is one of his own nightshirts. In the end he is compelled to believe that he did steal the Moonstone and that Rachel saw him doing so, though he has no recollection of doing so nor any idea what has become of it. He realizes too that although Rachel still loves him she will never forgive him.

Franklin is extricated from this apparently hopeless predicament by recourse to what amounts to psychopathology. A Doctor Candy, one of the guests at Rachel's dinner-party, fell ill shortly afterwards and became delirious. During his illness he was nursed by his assistant, Doctor Jennings, whose interest in brain physiology led him to take Candy's delirious wanderings down in shorthand. He did so in the hope of confirming his belief that it was possible to demonstrate the existence of an underlying logical train of thought in the apparently meaningless wanderings of delirious patients. He also wanted to test the hypothesis that 'every sensory impression which has once been recognised by the perceptive consciousness is registered in the brain and may be reproduced at some subsequent time, although there may be no consciousness in the mind in the whole intermediate period'. (In working out this part of the plot Collins quotes from the writings of Elliotson, the first professor of Medicine at University College Hospital, who was forced to resign his chair on account of his pioneering interest in hypnotism and medical psychology (cf. Flugel, 1933).)

Jennings's experiment is successful. His study of the 'free associations' he has recorded leads him to believe that while Doctor Candy was delirious he was trying to confess that after the dinner party he had poured 25 minims of laudanum into Franklin's brandy. He had done this in order to avenge himself for some slighting remarks on the medical profession that Franklin had made during dinner. Incidentally, Candy's action was not as malicious as it sounds; Franklin had mentioned during the evening that he had been sleeping badly and Candy wished to demonstrate his ability to relieve him.

As soon as Franklin gets this information from Jennings, the mystery is solved. Franklin stole the Moonstone while in a somnambulistic trance induced by his having unwittingly taken a considerable dose of opium. According to Jennings, who like Collins himself was something of an expert in such matters, his sensitivity to opium was due to his having been in a state of 'nervous irritation' produced by his having given up cigar-smoking during his courtship of Rachel, while his motive in stealing the diamond was his apprehension lest someone else should take it. Unfortunately, Godfrey Ablewhite, another cousin of Rachel's, who was sleeping in a room adjoining Franklin's, followed him when he went to Rachel's room, saw him take the Moonstone, realized that he was sleepwalking and stole it from him when he fell again into a deep sleep. Like Franklin, Ablewhite was also courting Rachel, but unlike Franklin his motives were purely mercenary. Ablewhite is murdered in his attempts to dispose of the Moonstone, but the jewel is never recovered. After the mystery is solved the lovers are reconciled and marry. The novel ends with the announcement that Rachel is pregnant. The girl who has lost her Moonstone for ever is about to acquire a child.

It is not, I think, necessary for me to demonstrate in detail that the theft of the Moonstone is a symbolic representation of the as yet prohibited intercourse between Franklin and Rachel and the loss of Rachel's virginity, nor to point out the symbolism of the Moonstone itself, with its central flaw and lunar changes in lustre, of the drawer in the Indian cabinet, of the decorative painting and the stain on the nightshirt, nor of the fact that Franklin gave up cigar-smoking during his courtship of Rachel. Nor need I analyse the reasons underlying Rachel's mother's concern for the safety of the Moonstone and Rachel's angry silence after the theft that she could so easily have prevented. All this is sufficiently obvious.

Instead I should like to discuss the theme of *The Moonstone* from a rather different angle, starting from a sociological or historical observation. *The Moonstone* was written in the late eighteen-sixties and purports to describe events occurring in an upper-middle-class setting some twenty years earlier. Now this was a time and an environment in which what later came to be called the 'double standard' of morality operated in theory if not entirely in practice. Young women of good family were assumed to be without sexual feelings and were expected to be not only innocent but also ignorant when they married. Her future husband however could, perhaps even should, have had sexual relationships with women from outside his own class. For the man, therefore, women were divided into two categories; those of his own class, who were idealized, one of whom he must eventually love and marry but must never think of sexually until after marriage; and those outside his own class, who were depreciated and with whom he could have sexual relationships but must never love and marry. This situation is virtually explicit in *The Moonstone*. Franklin is openly depicted as a young man with experience of the world and of women, while Rachel is an innocent girl of 18. She is, however, proud, high-spirited and independent-minded, a woman who might, one surmises, have difficulty in making the type of submissive surrender which the Victorian male, in theory at least, demanded of his wife. I mention this in view of the well-known unconscious connexion between loss of virginity and renunciation of the fantasy of having a penis (Freud, 1918).

If one views *The Moonstone* from the masculine point of view, the theft can be interpreted as a symbolic or symptomatic act or dream of a man in sexual conflict. Accustomed to sexual relationships with women outside his own class, he falls in love with his cousin whom he wishes to marry. Her status as an idealized non-sexual woman makes her, however, unavailable as an object of either sexual activity or fantasy. As a result he gives up cigar-smoking and suffers from insomnia and nervous irritation, i.e. he develops an actual neurosis. Then under the influence of opium he performs an act which is a symbolic fulfilment of his unadmitted wishes. The author exonerates him from guilt —and here the novel falls short of what I earlier called the ideal detective story—by providing him with a respectable, altruistic motive and by having the Moonstone re-stolen from him. Ablewhite, the scapegoat, is, however, obviously a personification of Franklin's own unconscious impulses. Franklin and Ablewhite are both maternal first cousins of Rachel and on the night of the crime they sleep in adjoining rooms. Ablewhite is also depicted as living according to the double standard, but unlike Franklin he does so hypocritically. He lives two lives, one with his mistress whom he maintains in luxury in the suburbs, the other as the devoted attendant on fashionable women in town and the secretary of numerous women's charitable organizations. Unlike Franklin he is prepared to degrade the idealized woman by marrying her for money.

Rachel's unconscious connivance in the crime can be interpreted in a complementary fashion. She falls in love with Franklin but her upbringing makes her blind to the physical aspects of being in love and to the problems and hazards that attach to the attainment of physical maturity. As a result she denies that there is any risk of the Moonstone being stolen— 'Are there thieves in the house?'—but when she sees her lover stealing it she is powerless to stop him and yet overcome with fury and mortification at his having done so; even though she remains intensely in love with him. This ambivalent reaction is reminiscent of the outburst of hostility that the woman may feel towards the man to whom she loses her virginity and which Freud discussed at length in his paper on the Taboo of Virginity.

Like Franklin, Rachel also has a double, who personifies her repressed sexuality. Her maid, Rosanna, who is a reformed thief and the daughter of a prostitute, falls in love with Franklin at first sight and shows all the signs of physical infatuation with him. She is the first, excepting Rachel, to realize that the Moonstone has been stolen and it is she who discovers that the missing stained garment is Franklin's nightshirt. Her love for Franklin leads her to suppress this vital clue and so she shares with Rachel the responsibility for making the theft of the Moonstone a mystery. The different motives that the author attributes to Rachel and Rosanna for their silence and suppression of evidence provide an interesting contrast. Rachel is actuated by injured pride; she is disgusted with herself for loving a man who has proved himself capable of such an ignoble act. Her maid has simpler and more straightforward motives; she loves and wishes to protect him. She also wishes to hold on to something which might enable her to make Franklin, who has always been oblivious of her as a person, notice her and be indebted to her. So far from being shocked by discovering that Franklin is the thief, she is quite prepared to use her former contacts with the criminal world to help him dispose of the Moonstone. She also considers quite realistically the possibility that there may have been sexual reasons for Franklin's presence in Rachel's room on the night of the crime.

In view of these considerations I suggest then not only that the theme of *The Moonstone* is an unconscious representation of a sexual act, but also that its four leading characters, Franklin, Ablewhite, Rachel and Rosanna represent different aspects of the sexual conflicts that arose in a society which sanctioned the tendency of the man to deal with his oedipal conflicts by dissociation and the creation of two opposed classes and conceptions of woman, one idealized and asexual, the other degraded and sexual. That the conflict underlying this tendency to dissociation does in fact stem from the Oedipus complex and the taboo on incest is represented by the fact that Franklin, Ablewhite, and Rachel, the three upper-class characters, are all first cousins. Franklin and Rachel are indeed described as having, as small children been brought up together as brother and sister.

One of the pitfalls of psycho-analytical interpretations of literary works is the fallacy of attributing to fictional characters unconscious motivations and conflicts, which can in fact only legitimately be attributed to their creator. I would at moments appear to have been guilty of this fallacy inasmuch as I have interpreted the theft of the Moonstone in terms of Rachel's and Franklin's sexual conflicts without relating these to Wilkie Collins's own psychology. I have, as it were, interpreted a dream in terms of the figures who appear in the dream without reference to the dreamer himself. In fact my interpretation of the novel presupposes three assumptions about Wilkie Collins himself:

(i) that there were in his mind certain specific constellations which compelled him in his writing to give symbolic expression to an unconscious preoccupation with the primal scene;

(ii) that idealization, splitting of the object, and projection were among the defences he used in his attempts to master anxiety; and

(iii) that he was preoccupied with virginity.

It must be admitted at once that it is impossible to support these assumptions about Wilkie Collins's psychopathology by direct biographical material. This is due not only to the general difficulties which naturally attach to any attempt to reconstruct the psychology of a man who was born in 1824 and died in 1889 but also to a specific one, the fact that Wilkie Collins was a very secretive man who, his biographer (Robinson, 1951) suggests, probably wished the story of his life to remain a mystery and took active steps to ensure that it did.

The manifest theme of another of his novels provides, however, evidence which very strongly suggests that the interpretation I have made of the latent content of *The Moonstone* is a correct one. The novel in question is *Basil*, which was published in 1852, sixteen years before *The Moonstone* and must have been written when Collins was aged 27 or 28. In his preface to it Collins wrote 'I have formed the main event out of which this story springs, on a fact within my own knowledge'. His biographer thinks it probable that the novel is based on an actual emotional experience of Collins himself and that he wrote it as a form of catharsis.

Basil is the younger son of an aristocrat who is inordinately proud of his ancient lineage. His mother died when he was a child but he has an only sister, Clara, to whom he is devoted. One day he falls in love at first sight with a tradesman's daughter, Margaret, a girl of 17. The night after he first sees her he has the following dream:

> This is what I dreamed:
> I stood on a wide plain. On one side it was bounded by thick woods, whose dark secret depths looked unfathomable to the eye; on the other by hills, ever rising higher and higher yet, until they were lost in bright, beautifully white clouds, gleaming in refulgent sunlight. On the side above the woods the sky was dark and vaporous. It seemed as if some thick exhalation had arisen from beneath the trees, and overspread the clear firmament throughout this portion of the scene.
> As I still stood on the plain and looked around, I saw a woman coming towards me from the wood. Her stature was tall; her black hair flowed about her unconfined, in wondrous luxuriance; her robe was of the dun hue of the vapour and mist which hung above the trees, and fell to her feet in dark, thick folds. She came on towards me swiftly and softly, passing over the ground like cloud-shadows over the ripe corn-field or the calm water.
> I looked to the other side, towards the hills, and there was

another woman descending from their bright summits, and her robe was white, and pure, and glistening. Her face was illumined with a light like the light of the harvest moon. and her footsteps, as she descended the hills, left a long track of brightness that sparkled far behind her, like the track of the stars when the winter night is clear and cold. She came to the place where the hills and the plain were joined together. Then she stopped, and I knew that she was watching me from afar off.

Meanwhile, the woman from the dark wood still approached, never pausing on her path, like the woman from the fair hills. And now I could see her face plainly. Her eyes were lustrous and fascinating, as the eyes of a serpent—large, dark, and soft, as the eyes of the wild doe. Her lips were parted with a languid smile, and she drew back the long hair which lay over her cheeks, her neck, her bosom, while I was gazing on her.

Then I felt as if a light were shining on me from the other side, so I turned round to look, and there was the woman from the hills beckoning me away to ascend with her towards the bright clouds above. Her arm, as she held it forth, shone fair, even against the fair hills, and from her outstretched hand came long, thin rays of trembling light, which penetrated to where I stood, cooling and calming wherever they touched me.

But the woman from the woods still came nearer and nearer, until I could feel her hot, panting breath on my face. Her eyes looked into mine and fascinated them, as she held out her arms to embrace me. I touched her hand, and in an instant the touch ran through me like fire, from head to foot. Then, still looking intently on me with her wild bright eyes, she clasped her supple arms round my neck and drew me a few paces away with her towards the wood.

I felt the rays of light that had touched me from the beckoning hand depart, and yet once more I looked towards the woman from the hills. She was ascending again towards the bright clouds, and ever and anon she stopped and turned round, wringing her hands and letting her head droop, as if in bitter grief. The last time I saw her look towards me she was near the clouds. She covered her face with her robe, and knelt down where she stood. After this I discerned no more of her, for now the woman from the wood clasped me more closely than before, pressing her warm lips on mine, and it was as if her long hair fell all around us both, spreading over my eyes like a veil, to hide from them the fair hill-tops and the woman who was walking onward to the bright clouds above.

Then I was drawn along in the arms of the dark woman, with my blood burning and my breath failing me, until we entered the secret recesses that lay amid the unfathomable depths of trees. And there she encircled me in the folds of her dusky robe and laid her hot cheek close to mine and murmured a mysterious music in my ear, amid the midnight silence and darkness of all that was around us. And I had no thought of returning to the plain again, for I had forgotten the woman from the fair hills and had given myself up, heart, and soul, and body, to the woman from the dark woods.

Here the dream ended, and I awoke.

After waking up he realizes at once that the two women in the dream are Margaret and Clara and that his infatuation for Margaret has overwhelmed him. Loyalty to his father's and Clara's ideals no longer has any power to restrain him. He calls on Margaret's father, asks him for her hand in marriage, and owing to the impossibility of this breach of the family standards ever being condoned by his father, he marries her secretly. Margaret's father however attaches a condition to the secret marriage, which is that it shall not be consummated for a year. Basil makes no attempt to break this condition and sees her only in the presence of a chaperone. During this time he ignores the numerous clues which could have told him that Margaret, though beautiful, is worthless and interested only in his position and fortune, not in himself. Nor does he heed various warnings from Margaret's mother that he is in danger from her father's confidential clerk, Mannion, a single man in his early forties. On the 364th night of the unconsummated marriage Basil sees Margaret and Mannion alight from a carriage and enter a hotel together. He follows them, hides in an adjoining room and hears Mannion seduce Margaret.

I listened, and through the thin partition, I heard voices—*her* voice and *his* voice. *I heard and I knew*—knew my degradation in all its infamy, knew my wrongs in all their nameless horror.

After this dramatic moment the novel becomes increasingly melodramatic. Basil attacks Mannion as he comes out of the hotel, leaving him half-dead and hideously disfigured for life. Basil returns home where he has a nervous breakdown, during the course of which he works over the events of the previous year, re-experiencing every incident which, had he not been blinded by infatuation, could have told him Margaret's and Mannion's true characters. Mannion is taken to hospital, where he is visited by Margaret who catches typhus from another patient. Basil is present at his wife's deathbed, where this time it is Mannion who listens from an adjoining room. It is at this point perhaps relevant to mention that Collins wrote *The Moonstone* while his mother was dying and he was too ill with gout to be with her. Basil and Mannion meet at Margaret's grave, where Mannion vows that he will pursue Basil for the rest of his life, making him an outcast wherever he goes. 'Go where you will, this face of mine shall never be turned away from you'. Basil flees to a remote village in Cornwall, a county he associates with an adored nurse of his childhood. Mannion is true to his vow and within three weeks Basil realizes that the villagers have turned against him. 'We want you gone from here because we want our children's faces left as God made them'.

However Basil is spared a life time's persecution and the reader is given a happy ending, as Mannion very conveniently falls into a chasm set in the Cornish cliffs. Basil had been walking along the cliffs in a mood of despair and Mannion had been following him to make sure that he would not escape from vengeance by committing suicide.

It is, I think, again unnecessary for me to underline the obvious and to demonstrate in detail the similarities between the manifest plot of *Basil* and the latent theme of *The Moonstone*. I should perhaps however say something more about Mannion, who is in some ways the key character in *Basil*. Not only is he obviously a representative of Margaret's father, whose confidential clerk he is, but various details make it possible to establish a connexion between him and both Basil and Basil's father. Mannion, despite his present humble station in life, is himself by origin an aristocrat and is the son of a friend of Basil's father, whose betrayal of him was responsible for Mannion's father being hanged and for Mannion becoming an outcast from society. Mannion's persecution of Basil is not only revenge for Basil having used his social position to steal the girl he had hoped to marry and for the disfigurement he suffered at Basil's hands after the seduction; it is also his revenge for the injury Basil's father had done to him and his father. Mannion, however, resembles Basil's father in at least two respects; pride is the actuating motive in both their lives and both are incapable of forgiveness. If one compares *The Moonstone* and *Basil*, Mannion plays in *Basil* the rôle which is equivalent to that played by Ablewhite in *The Moonstone*; they are the scapegoats, the representatives and agents of the heroes' unadmitted impulses, and, as always happens to scapegoats, they both die as an indirect result of the crimes they commit. However, they are not only personifications of the 'bad' aspects of the heroes, Basil and Franklin; they are also representations of the fathers of the participants in the central crime. In *Basil*, in which the underlying pathology is relatively undisguised, Mannion is both a projection of Margaret's sexual imago of her father and a projection, at one and the same time, of Basil's father and Basil's hostility to his father. In other words the relationship between Mannion and Margaret is oedipal, both from Margaret's and Basil's standpoint. In *The Moonstone*, the identification of Ablewhite with Franklin's and Rachel's father is only hinted at. In fact fathers are conspicuous by their absence, Ablewhite being the only character who even has one. However Ablewhite has an identical relationship to both Franklin and Rachel, since he is first cousin to both, while in *Basil*, Mannion and Basil have what could be thought of as a disguised cousin-relationship; they are sons of erstwhile bosom friends.

Before leaving the plots of these two novels, I should like to draw attention to two curious minor details. The first is that the mothers of both Margaret and Rachel give warnings which go unheeded. The second is that, although *The Moonstone* was written in 1867-8, the events in it are represented as having occurred in 1848-50, i.e. in the years immediately preceding the publication of *Basil* in 1852. As there seems to be no reason intrinsic to the plot for this, it is tempting to think that it is not an accident that Collins set the theft of the Moonstone during the period in which he must have had the experience which led him to write *Basil* as a form of catharsis.

If one views these two novels together as studies in the psychopathology of the double standard, *Basil* can be seen as the reverse of *The Moonstone*. *The Moonstone* deals with the conflict aroused by the emergence of repressed sexual feelings towards the idealized object, *Basil* with the conflict produced by the alternative but inadmissible attempt at resolution, idealization of the inferior, degraded sexual object. It is not surprising that *Basil* shocked most of its readers when it first appeared, and that it is only *The Moonstone* that has retained its popularity.

In conclusion, I should like to quote one of the few known anecdotes of Wilkie Collins's childhood:

When he was only twelve years old he conceived a passionate affection for a married woman three times his age. So intense was his jealousy of the woman's husband that he could not bear to be in the same room and ran away whenever he saw him approaching. (Robinson, 1951.)

10

The Effect of the Psychoneurotic Patient on his Environment[1]

The only environment of which the analyst of a psychoneurotic has any certain knowledge is the setting within which psycho-analytical treatment takes place, this setting comprising the room in which the analyst and patient meet and the analyst himself in it, and the analyst, instead of allowing the patient to have any effect on his room or himself, adopts a particular tech-nical procedure, viz. interpretation, in order to prevent any effects that the patient intends from actually occurring. As a result, it could be argued, the analyst is doubly disqualified from discussing the effect of the psychoneurotic on his environment. First, he never sees the environment in which the patient lives out his illness and therefore never knows what effect his patient actually has, even though he may know a lot about what the patient is trying to do to his spouse, parents, friends, etc., and may also know a lot about what the patient imagines he is doing; but the analyst has no direct knowledge of what the effects actually are, or of what resistance or compliance the psychoneurotic's efforts actually encounter. Secondly, he adopts a technique, that of interpretation, which precludes 'effects on the environment', at any rate in the ordinary, expected sense of the phrase, from occurring within the environment in which he does see the patient.

However, I do not in fact consider that as an analyst I am disqualified from contributing anything germane to this dis-cussion. My reason for believing that, on the contrary, a psycho-analyst has something important to say about the effect of the psychoneurotic on his environment, derives from my conviction that the analyst–patient relationship is one in which certain aspects of human interaction can be studied under conditions of

[1] Paper presented to the Conference on the Rôle of Psychosomatic Disorder in Adult Life held on 3–4 November 1961, and published in the Proceedings of that Conference, entitled *The Rôle of Psychosomatic Disorder in Adult Life*, ed. Wisdom and Wolff (Oxford: Pergamon, 1965).

relative isolation from the network of social complications which obscure and confuse all 'real-life' relationships. Study of the analyst–patient relationship should therefore, I believe, provide insight into the nature of the forces within the psychoneurotic which compel him to have a pathogenic effect upon his environment, and also into the nature of the factors which determine to what extent individuals in his environment will succumb to or resist these forces. It will not however provide objective or quantifiable evidence as to the effect which the psychoneurotic population as a whole has on its environment, or as to the incidence of particular neurotic combinations and constellations within families and other naturally occurring groups. Facts of this kind can only be ascertained by direct observation.

The effect that any individual, whether neurotic or otherwise, has on persons in his environment is a function of at least four factors. First, the nature of the social, legal and biological ties existing between the persons involved; secondly, the strength or energy that the individual has available for imposing his conscious and unconscious wishes upon his objects; thirdly, the nature of the various rôles that he wishes persons in his environment to play; and fourthly, the susceptibility of the persons in his environment to be affected by his psychology. In the remainder of this paper I intend to discuss the effect of the psychoneurotic on his environment on the basis of these four factors; for simplicity of exposition I shall confine myself to two-person relationships and shall talk as though the psychoneurotic's environment consisted of a number of unconnected relationships with single individuals. Here again I am influenced by the fact that the psycho-analytical situation only permits direct observation of the patient's attitude towards a single individual.

It is obvious that a psychoneurotic can only have an effect on another person insofar as some tie exists between the two and that the nature of the effect will be limited by the nature of the tie, and that the extent of the effect will vary directly with the degree of indissolubility of the tie. The example most frequently mentioned in the literature is the fact that the susceptibility of children to be affected by neurotogenic or schizophrenogenic mothers is dependent on the inherent strength of the tie between a child and its mother and on the fact that a child has no conceivable avenue of escape and has a very restricted choice of alternative objects. It is however also true that the capacity of neurotic children to drive their parents frantic depends on the ties which prevent parents escaping from their children; and that the capacity of one spouse to have a pathogenic effect on the other depends on the extent to which economic, legal and moral considerations prevent the threatened spouse from taking evasive action. It would indeed be interesting to know how early, and to what extent, children can put their parents into the 'double bind' described by Bateson *et al.* (1956), and to what extent rigid social systems permit adults to do the same to one another. In the psycho-analytical situation this matter of the tie can also become important, since both the transference and the counter-transference are influenced by the extent to which the two parties to the relationship regard the other as irreplaceable or inescapable.

The strength or energy that any neurotic has available to impose himself on another depends on many factors and I doubt whether we possess any satisfactory explanation as to why neurotics vary so enormously in their capacity to impose themselves on others. One can, it is true, enumerate some of the techniques used, such as manipulation of the object's unconscious sense of guilt, overt or concealed sexual seductiveness, infantile charm and importunity, all of which depend to a greater or lesser extent on the neurotic possessing an unconscious understanding of the unconscious of others, but none of these factors really explains why some neurotics are by and large successful in finding objects to collude with them and people to help them, while others are pathetically ineffectual. In his paper on the Special Patient Main (1957) has described a type of neurotic who is conspicuously successful in provoking doctors into making heroic therapeutic endeavours on his or her behalf, but so far as I know no-one has discussed the reasons why some neurotics appear to be incapable of exciting anyone's therapeutic interest. Presumably this difference depends partly on the individual's total vitality, which is a biological, constitutional factor, partly on how much energy is available for external relations after expenditure on intra-psychic conflict, and partly on the extent to which the individual's psychopathology centres on the fantasy of some ideal object who will support, satisfy or save him. The enormous energy frequently displayed by hysterics of all sexes in compelling others to play predetermined rôles in their life certainly depends on their capacity to defend themselves against intra-psychic conflict, guilt, and depression by sustaining the fantasy of an ideal rescuing, all-providing object. In analysis of such patients the analyst has to be able to resist the patient's pressure to make him play simultaneously the rôles of Great Mother, Jesus Christ, and Rudolph Valentino, and to remain immune to the flattery implicit in being cast for such a glamorous rôle. When, as sometimes happens, the therapist falls for this interpretation of his rôle, the explanation lies in collusion between the patient's passive belief in an omnipotent object and the therapist's own active omnipotent fantasies.

When we come to consider the nature of the various rôles which the neurotic wishes to impose on his objects, we are on surer ground, since these rôles, and the accompanying infantile wishes, are deducible from his psychopathology and reveal themselves in the analytical situation as transference. Insofar as the neurotic is infantilely dependent, he will attempt to turn his analyst into a supporting parent, and in real life he will attempt to do the same to his objects. If he is phobic, he will envisage the analytical situation as the one haven in a dangerous world; in real life, home and one person in it will alone be trusted. If he is 'castrating', the analyst will have to interpret the patient's wish to make him feel small, incompetent and ineffectual. Outside the session, others will feel the same pressure. If he is obsessional, he will try to mechanize and control the analyst; in everyday life his objects will similarly feel their spontaneity threatened. If he is hysterical, he will idealize the analyst and then feel betrayed if the analyst rejects this rôle. And so on; in each and every case the transference reveals the rôle which the psychoneurotic wishes his objects to play. In the analytical situation his object, the analyst, refuses to play this rôle and instead interprets, so that the effect aimed at is not achieved, and the patient acquires insight instead of collusion.

In his real life environment, however, the neurotic's wish to impose predetermined rôles on his objects is unlikely to encounter the same sort of mutative resistance as it meets in the analytical situation. Although he may meet and become involved with persons who possess insight, a commodity in which analysts certainly have no monopoly, only rarely will such persons be in a position to give the neurotic more than a limited amount of help; the nature of the relationship, the kind of tie binding them to the patient, usually precludes the possibility of their making use of the various technical devices, such as fixed sessions, which psychotherapists use to maintain a certain distance between themselves and their patients. However, neurotics do on occasion become involved in what one might call spontaneous semi-therapeutic relationships, usually with persons much older than themselves.

However, despite the fact that psychoneurotics rarely encounter individuals in their environment who by training or temperament are capable of turning the relationship to therapeutic effect, it would, I believe, be a mistake to suppose that they are uniformly successful in compelling their objects to fit in with their neurotic tendencies. Although one may from time to time come across examples of extraordinarily complete collusion between two neurotics, to take such occurrences as paradigmatic of the psychoneurotic's effect on his environment would be as misguided as to assume that *folie à deux* is typical of the psychotic's relationship to his environment. The extent of the pathogenic effect exerted by the neurotic is limited not only by the differences in susceptibility of his objects, which I shall discuss later, but also by factors in his own personality.

These factors derive from the fact that the psychoneurotic is not totally ill. By definition a psychoneurotic is a person who has a perceptible amount of stability, insight and integrity, and one can assume therefore that the extent to which his neurotic tendencies are allowed to impinge on his objects will be limited, to a greater or lesser extent, by himself. His good sense, his concern for others, his sense of humour, will prevent his taking his tendency to 'act out' to the absolute limit. Despite the fact that some neurotics are experts in brinkmanship, one makes, I think, a mistake if one assumes that psychoneurotics go round being ill all the time, perpetually unloading their illnesses on their nearest and ambivalently dearest. In the analytical situation, the stability and health of the neurotic is shown by his willing co-operation in transforming wishes into insight.

The susceptibility of any individual in a neurotic's environment to be pathogenically affected by him depends on the same factors which in general determine to what extent any individual is impressionable or resistant to the influence of others. In discussing these factors one has first to distinguish between rigidity and stability. Rigid persons are those whose equilibrium depends on characterological defences, i.e. defences which have become part of the personality, into which they have no insight, and which compel them to be impervious and unresponsive to the nuances of mood, feeling and desire in those around them. Such persons, so far from being affected by neurotics around them, affect them. It is possible that such persons play an aetiological rôle in the history of every neurotic illness; this at least is the implication of most studies of family interaction. Or if rigid persons are affected by a psychoneurotic it is in the direction of making them more rigid (cf. Laing, 1961).

Stable persons, on the other hand, can afford to be influenced by the feelings and desires of those around them and are therefore liable to be affected by a psychoneurotic. These effects can be divided into three categories. First, reactions of concern and helpfulness, which depend on the individual having recognized that the neurotic is ill and in trouble. Secondly, reactions of self-protection designed to prevent the individual becoming confused by the disordered moods and behaviour of the neurotic. Thirdly, reactions dependent upon suggestibility, by which I mean the tendency to accept rôles which are overtly or covertly offered to one, to identify with the rôles which others are projecting on to one. It is on the psychology of this last, third reaction, that the pathogenic effects of the neurotic on his environment really depends. The reactions of concern and self-protection can be regarded as normal responses outside the scope of this discussion.

The capacity to empathise and identify with others, and to accept rôles offered to one, is in itself a normal psychic function which plays an intrinsic part in individual development and which contributes to the formation and maintenance of every personal relationship. Yet phenomena such as hypnosis, *folie à deux* and infatuations show that this function or mechanism can operate in such a way as to threaten the individual's identity and render him liable to intrusions, projections and manipulations by others. Although susceptibility to such occurrences can up to a point be regarded as a normal hazard of interpersonal relations, the analytical situation affords opportunities of gaining insight into some of the factors which may exaggerate this susceptibility and render the individual liable to pathological involvement in the illnesses of others. One is provided by those occasions on which the therapist identifies himself excessively with the patient and feels tempted to play the rôle being demanded of him. Another is provided by patients who construct all their relationships on an identificatory basis, who absorb the mannerisms of their objects, and whose transference is characterized by idealization and imitation of their analyst. Analysis of the former shows that part at least of the therapist's therapeutic drive originates in the need to understand childhood objects who were hated and feared, while analysis of the latter shows that their psychic development was overshadowed by the fantasy of an omnipotent, overpowering 'bad' object, to whom accommodation could only be made by submission, identification, and surrender of personal identity. The common feature in the two cases is that the mechanism of identification has been defensively used as a defence against hated and feared objects, and not as a means of assimilating the characteristics of loved ones.

If one applies these analytical findings to the effect of the psychoneurotic patient on his environment, one reaches the conclusion that the susceptibility of his objects to pathogenic influence depends on the extent to which they use identification as a defence against their hostility to him, and, to put it the other way round, that the extent to which any individual colludes with a neurotic, or allows himself to be manipulated or 'had on' by one, depends on how hostile or frightened he is and on the extent to which he uses 'identification with the aggressor', to use Anna Freud's phrase, as a defence. This will, of course, not depend solely on how provoking or frightening the neurotic himself is, but also on the extent to which he experiences the neurotic as a reincarnation of his own infantile 'bad' objects.

References

Abraham, K. (1913. 'A constitutional basis of locomotor anxiety.' In: *Selected Papers of Karl Abraham* (London: Hogarth, 1927, 1942, 1950; New York: Basic Books, 1953).

—— (1933). 'A short study of the development of the libido.' *ibid.*

Balint, A. (1944). 'Über eine besondere Form der infantilen Angst.' *Zeit. f. psychoanal Pädagogik*, 7 (Abstract in *Int. J. Psycho-Anal.*, 15).

Balint, M. (1952). *Primary Love and Psycho-Analytic Technique* (London: Hogarth; new edition: Tavistock, 1966).

Bateson, G., et al. (1956). 'Toward a theory of schizophrenia.' *Behavioral Sci.*, 1.

Best and Taylor (1939). *The Physiological Basis of Medical Practice* (London: Baillière).

Bonaparte, M. (1933). *The Life and Works of Edgar Allan Poe* (London: Imago, 1949).

Bowlby, J. (1952). 'Instinct and object relation theories of zoologists.' Unpublished paper read to the British Psycho-Analytical Society.

—— (1958). 'The nature of the child's tie to his mother.' *Int. J. Psycho-Anal.*, 39.

—— (1960a). 'Separation anxiety' *Int. J. Psycho-Anal.*, 41.

—— (1960b). 'Grief and mourning in infancy and early childhood.' *Psychoanal. Study Child*, 15.

Brierley, M. (1951). *Trends in Psycho-Analysis* (London: Hogarth).

Collins, Wilkie (1852). *Basil* (London: Bentley).

—— (1868). *The Moonstone* (Harmondsworth: Penguin, 1955).

Eder, D. (1932). 'The myth of progress' In. *David Eder*, ed. Hobman (London: Gollancz).

Eliot, T. S. (1921). 'Metaphysical poets.' In: *Selected Essays* (London: Faber).

Fenichel, O. (1939). 'The counterphobic attitude.' *Int. J. Psycho-Anal.*, 20.

—— (1945). *The Psychoanalytic Theory of Neurosis* (New York: Norton).

Fliess, R. (1953). *The Revival of Interest in the Dream* (New York: Int. Univ. Press).

Flugel, J. C. (1933). *A Hundred Years of Psychology* (London: Duckworth).

Forster, E. M. (1910). *Howard's End*, Chapter 12 (London: Arnold).

French, T. M. (1929). 'Psychogenic material related to the function of the semicircular canals.' *Int. J. Psycho-Anal.*, 10.

REFERENCES

Freud, A. (1936). *The Ego and the Mechanisms of Defence* (London: Hogarth, 1937; New York: Int. Univ. Press, 1946).

Freud, S. (1910). 'The psychoanalytic view of psychogenic visual disturbance.' *Standard Edition of the Complete Psychological Works of Sigmund Freud*, **11**.

—— (1911*a*). 'Psycho-analytic notes on an autobiographical account of a case of paranoia (dementia paranoides).' *Standard Edition*, **12**.

—— (1911*b*). 'Formulations on the two principles of mental functioning.' *Standard Edition*, **12**.

—— (1915). 'The unconscious.' *Standard Edition*, **14**.

—— (1916–17). *Introductory Lectures on Psycho-Analysis, Standard Edition*, **15–16**.

——(1918). The taboo of virginity.' *Standard Edition*, **11**.

—— (1923). *The Ego and the Id. Standard Edition*, **19**.

—— (1933). *New Introductory Lectures on Psycho-Analysis. Standard Edition*, **22**.

Hartmann, H. (1939). *Ego Psychology and the Problem of Adaptation* (New York: Int. Univ. Press, 1958; London: Hogarth, 1959).

Hermann, I. (1936). 'Sick-Anklammern—Auf-Suche-Gehen.' *Int. Z. f. Psychoanal.*, **22** (Abstract in *Int. J. Psycho-Anal.*, **18**).

Hull, L. W. H. (1959). *The History and Philosophy of Science* (London: Longman).

Isaacs, S. (1948). 'The nature and function of phantasy.' *Int. J. Psycho-Anal.*, **29**.

Isakower, O. (1938). 'A contribution to the patho-psychology of phenomena associated with falling asleep.' *Int. J. Psycho-Anal.*, **19**.

Jespersen, O. (1922). *Language: Its Nature, Development and Origin* (London: Allen & Unwin).

Jones, E. (1911). 'The relationship between dreams and psychoneurotic symptoms.' *Papers on Psycho-Analysis* (London: Baillière, 1st edition 1913—fifth edition, 1948).

—— (1916). 'The theory of symbolism.' *ibid.*, 2nd edition 1918 onwards.

Klein, M. (1930). 'The importance of symbol formation in the development of the ego.' *Contributions to Psycho-Analysis* (London: Hogarth, 1948).

—— (1935). 'A contribution to the psychogenesis of manic-depressive states.' *ibid.*

Kubie, L. S. (1953). 'The distortion of the symbolic process in neurosis and psychosis.' *J. Amer. Psychoanal. Assoc.*, **1**.

Laing, R. D. (1961). *The Self and Others* (London: Tavistock).

Langer, S. (1942). *Philosophy in a New Key* (London: Oxford Univ. Press; Cambridge, Mass.: Harvard Univ. Press, 1951).

Leiri, F. (1927). 'Uber den Schwindel.' *Zeit. Hals, Nasen u. Ohrenheilkunde*, **17**.

Lewin, B. D. (1946). 'Sleep, the mouth and the dream screen.' *Psychoanal. Quart.*, **15**.

—— (1948). 'Inferences from the dream screen.' *Int. J. Psycho-Anal.*, **29**.

—— (1949). 'Mania and sleep.' *Psychoanal. Quart.*, **18**.

—— (1958). *Dreams and the Uses of Regression* (New York: Int. Univ. Press).

Lindemann, E. (1944). 'Symptomatology and management of acute grief.' *Amer. J. Psychiat.*, **101**.

Lorenz, M. (1953). 'Language as expressive behavior.' *Arch. Neurol. Psychiat.*, **70**.

Lorenz, M. and Cobb, S. (1953). 'Language behavior in psychoneurotic patients.' *Arch. Neurol. Psychiat.*, **69**.

Lynd, H. M. (1958). *On Shame and the Search for Identity* (London: Routledge).

McDougall, W. (1931). *An Introduction to Social Psychology*, 22nd edition, Chapters 5 and 6 (London: Methuen).

Madison, P. (1956). 'Freud's repression concept.' *Int. J. Psycho-Anal.*, **37**.

Main, T. (1957). 'The ailment.' *Brit. J. med. Psychol.*, **30**.

Milner, M. (1952). 'Aspects of symbolism in comprehension of the notself.' *Int. J. Psycho-Anal.*, **33**.

Ortega y Gasset, J. (1931). *The Modern Theme* (New York: Harper, 1961).

Pedersen-Krag, G. (1949). 'Detective stories and the primal scene.' *Psychoanal. Quart.*, **18**.

Rado, S. (1928). 'The problem of melancholia.' *Int. J. Psycho-Anal.*, **9**.

Rapaport, D. (1953). 'On the psycho-analytic theory of affects.' *Int. J. Psycho-Anal.*, **34**.

Ribble, M. A. (1943). *The Rights of Infants* (New York: Columbia Univ. Press).

Richards, I. A. (1934). *Coleridge: On Imagination* (London: Routledge).

Robinson, K. (1951). *Wilkie Collins* (London: Bodley Head).

Schilder, P. (1930). 'The unity of body, sadism and dizziness.' *Psychoanal. Rev.*, **17**.

—— (1935). *The Image and Appearance of the Human Body* (London: Paul, Trench, Trubner; New York: Int. Univ. Press, 1950).

—— (1939). 'The relations between clinging and equilibrium.' *Int. J. Psycho-Anal.*, **20**.

—— (1942). *Mind: Perception and Thought in their Constructive Aspects* (New York: Columbia Univ. Press).

REFERENCES

Segal, H. (1957). 'Notes on symbol formation.' *Int. J. Psycho.-Anal.*, **38**.

Sharpe, E. (1937). *Dream Analysis* (London: Hogarth, 1937).

Sharpe, E. (1940). 'Psycho-physical problems revealed in language: an examination of metaphor.' *Collected Papers on Psycho-Analysis* (London: Hogarth, 1950).

Sterba, R. (1934). 'The fate of the ego in analytic therapy.' *Int. J. Psycho-Anal.*, **15**.

Stone, L. (1947). 'Transference sleep in a neurosis with duodenal ulcer.' *Int. J. Psycho-Anal.*, **28**.

Tinbergen, N. (1953). *Social Behaviour in Animals* (London: Methuen).

Winnicott, D. W. (1945). 'Primitive emotional development.' *Collected Papers* (London: Tavistock, 1958).

Index

INDEX

142

INDEX